Michael H. Miner, PhD
Eli Coleman, PhD
Editors

Sex Offender Treatment: Accomplishments, Challenges, and Future Directions

Sex Offender Treatment: Accomplishments, Challenges, and Future Directions has been co-published simultaneously as *Journal of Psychology & Human Sexuality*, Volume 13, Numbers 3/4 2001.

Pre-publication REVIEWS, COMMENTARIES, EVALUATIONS . . .

"AN EASY-TO-READ COLLECTION that reviews the major issues and findings on the past decade of research on and treatment of sex offenders. The busy professional will find this book A QUICK AND HELPFUL UPDATE for their practice. The reviews presented are succinct, but capture the main issues to be addressed by anyone working with sex offenders."

R. Langevin, PhD, CPsych
Director, Juniper Psychological Services, and Associate Professor of Psychiatry, University of Toronto

The Haworth Press, Inc.

Sex Offender Treatment: Accomplishments, Challenges, and Future Directions

Sex Offender Treatment: Accomplishments, Challenges, and Future Directions has been co-published simultaneously as *Journal of Psychology & Human Sexuality*, Volume 13, Numbers 3/4 2001.

The *Journal of Psychology & Human Sexuality* Monographic "Separates"

Below is a list of "separates," which in serials librarianship means a special issue simultaneously published as a special journal issue or double-issue *and* as a "separate" hardbound monograph. (This is a format which we also call a "DocuSerial.")

"Separates" are published because specialized libraries or professionals may wish to purchase a specific thematic issue by itself in a format which can be separately cataloged and shelved, as opposed to purchasing the journal on an on-going basis. Faculty members may also more easily consider a "separate" for classroom adoption.

"Separates" are carefully classified separately with the major book jobbers so that the journal tie-in can be noted on new book order slips to avoid duplicate purchasing.

You may wish to visit Haworth's website at . . .

http://www.HaworthPress.com

. . . to search our online catalog for complete tables of contents of these separates and related publications.

You may also call 1-800-HAWORTH (outside US/Canada: 607-722-5857), or Fax 1-800-895-0582 (outside US/Canada: 607-771-0012), or e-mail at:

getinfo@haworthpressinc.com

Sex Offender Treatment: Accomplishments, Challenges, and Future Directions, edited by Michael H. Miner, PhD, and Eli Coleman, PhD (Vol. 13, No. 3/4, 2001). *AN EASY-TO-READ COLLECTION that reviews the major issues and findings on the past decade of research on and treatment of sex offenders. The busy professional will find this book A QUICK AND HELPFUL UPDATE for their practice. The reviews presented are succinct, but capture the main issues to be addressed by anyone working with sex offenders." (R. Langevin, PhD, CPsych, Director, Juniper Psychological Services and Associate Professor of Psychiatry, University of Toronto)*

Childhood Sexuality: Normal Sexual Behavior and Development, edited by Theo G. M. Sandfort, PhD, and Jany Rademakers, PhD (Vol. 12, No. 1/2, 2000). *"Important. . . . Gives voice to children about their own 'normal' sexual curiosities and desires, and about their behavior and development." (Gunter Schmidt, PhD, Professor, Department of Sex Research, University of Hamburg, Germany)*

Sexual Offender Treatment: Biopsychosocial Perspectives, edited by Eli Coleman, PhD, and Michael Miner, PhD (Vol. 10, No. 3, 2000). *"This guide delivers a diverse look at the complex and intriguing topic of normal child sexuality and the progress that is being made in this area of research."*

New International Directions in HIV Prevention for Gay and Bisexual Men, edited by Michael T. Wright, LICSW, B. R. Simon Rosser, PhD, MPH, and Onno de Zwart, MA (Vol. 10, No. 3/4, 1998). *"Performs a great service to HIV prevention research and health promotion. . . . It takes the words of gay and bisexual men seriously by locating men's sexual practice in their love relationships and casual sex encounters and examines their responses to HIV." (Susan Kippax, Associate Professor and Director, National Center in HIV Social Research, School of Behavioral Sciences, Macquarie University, New South Wales, Australia)*

Sexuality Education in Postsecondary and Professional Training Settings, edited by James W. Maddock (Vol. 9, No. 3/4, 1997). *"A diverse group of contributors–all experienced sexuality educators–offer summary information, critical commentary, thoughtful analysis, and projections of future trends in sexuality education in postsecondary settings. . . . The chapters present valuable resources, ranging from historical references to contemporary Web sites." (Adolescence)*

Sexual Coercion in Dating Relationships, edited by E. Sandra Byers and Lucia F. O'Sullivan (Vol. 8, No. 1/2, 1996). *"Tackles a big issue with the best tools presently available to social and health scientists. . . . Perhaps the most remarkable thing about these excellent chapters is the thread of optimism that remains despite the depressing topic. Each author. . . chips away at oppression and acknowledges the strength of women who have experienced sexual coercion while struggling to eliminate sexist assumptions that deny women sexual autonomy and pleasure." (Naomi B. McCormick, PhD, Professor, Department of Psychology, State University of New York at Plattsburgh)*

HIV/AIDS and Sexuality, edited by Michael W. Ross (Vol. 7, No. 1/2, 1995). *"An entire volume on the topic of HIV and sexuality, bringing together a number of essays and studies, which cover a wide range of relevant issues. It really is a relief to finally read some research and thoughts about sexual functioning and satisfaction in HIV-positive persons." (Association of Lesbian and Gay Psychologists)*

Gender Dysphoria: Interdisciplinary Approaches in Clinical Management, edited by Walter O. Bockting and Eli Coleman (Vol. 5, No. 4, 1993). *"A Useful Modern Summary of the State-of-the-Art Endocrine and Psychiatric Approach to this Important Problem." (Stephen B. Levine, MD, Clinical Professor of Psychiatry, School of Medicine, Case Western Reserve University; Co-Director, Center for Marital and Sexual Health)*

Sexual Transmission of HIV Infection: Risk Reduction, Trauma, and Adaptation, edited by Lena Nilsson Schönnesson, PhD (Vol. 5, No. 1/2, 1992). *"This is an essential title for understanding how AIDS and HIV are perceived and treated in modern America." (The Bookwatch)*

John Money: A Tribute, edited by Eli Coleman (Vol. 4, No. 2, 1991). *"Original, provocative, and breaks new ground." (Science Books & Films)*

Sex Offender Treatment: Accomplishments, Challenges, and Future Directions

Michael H. Miner, PhD
Eli Coleman, PhD
Editors

Sex Offender Treatment: Accomplishments, Challenges, and Future Directions has been co-published simultaneously as *Journal of Psychology & Human Sexuality*, Volume 13, Numbers 3/4 2001.

The Haworth Press, Inc.
New York • London • Oxford

Sex Offender Treatment: Accomplishments, Challenges, and Future Directions has been co-published simultaneously as *Journal of Psychology & Human Sexuality*™, Volume 13, Numbers 3/4 2001.

Cover design by Marylouise Doyle

The Haworth Press, Inc., 10 Alice Street, Binghamton, NY 13904-1580 USA

Library of Congress Cataloging-in-Publication Data

Sex offender treatment : accomplishments, challenges, and future directions / Michael H. Miner, Eli Coleman, editors.
     p. cm.
"Has also been published as Journal of psychology & human sexuality, volume 13, numbers 3/4 2001."
Includes bibliographical references and index.
    ISBN 0-7890-1982-5 (hard : alk. paper) – ISBN 0-7890-1983-3 (pbk. : alk. paper)
    1. Psychosexual disorders–Treatment. 2. Sex offenders. I. Miner, Michael, PhD. II. Coleman, Eli.
RC556 .S4725 2002
616.85'8306–dc21

                       2002010505

Indexing, Abstracting & Website/Internet Coverage

This section provides you with a list of major indexing & abstracting services. That is to say, each service began covering this periodical during the year noted in the right column. Most Websites which are listed below have indicated that they will either post, disseminate, compile, archive, cite or alert their own Website users with research-based content from this work. (This list is as current as the copyright date of this publication.)

Abstracting, Website/Indexing Coverage . . . . Year When Coverage Began

- *Cambridge Scientific Abstracts (Risk Abstracts) <www.csa.com>* . . . **1992**
- *CNPIEC Reference Guide: Chinese National Directory of Foreign Periodicals* **1995**
- *Educational Administration Abstracts (EAA)* **1995**
- *e-psyche, LLC <www.e-psyche.net>* **2001**
- *Family & Society Studies Worldwide <www.nisc.com>* **1996**
- *Family Violence & Sexual Assault Bulletin* **1991**
- *FINDEX <www.publist.com>* **1999**
- *Gay & Lesbian Abstracts <www.nisc.com>* **2000**
- *GenderWatch <www.slinfo.com>* **1999**
- *Higher Education Abstracts, providing the latest in research & theory in more than 140 major topics* **1991**
- *IBZ International Bibliography of Periodical Literature <www.saur.de>* **1996**
- *Index Guide to College Journals (core list compiled by integrating 48 indexes frequently used to support undergraduate programs in small to medium libraries)* **1999**
- *Index to Periodical Articles Related to Law* **1991**

(continued)

Special Bibliographic Notes related to special journal issues (separates) and indexing/abstracting:

- indexing/abstracting services in this list will also cover material in any "separate" that is co-published simultaneously with Haworth's special thematic journal issue or DocuSerial. Indexing/abstracting usually covers material at the article/chapter level.
- monographic co-editions are intended for either non-subscribers or libraries which intend to purchase a second copy for their circulating collections.
- monographic co-editions are reported to all jobbers/wholesalers/approval plans. The source journal is listed as the "series" to assist the prevention of duplicate purchasing in the same manner utilized for books-in-series.
- to facilitate user/access services all indexing/abstracting services are encouraged to utilize the co-indexing entry note indicated at the bottom of the first page of each article/chapter/contribution.
- this is intended to assist a library user of any reference tool (whether print, electronic, online, or CD-ROM) to locate the monographic version if the library has purchased this version but not a subscription to the source journal.
- individual articles/chapters in any Haworth publication are also available through the Haworth Document Delivery Service (HDDS).

Sex Offender Treatment: Accomplishments, Challenges, and Future Directions

CONTENTS

ABOUT THE EDITORS

Michael H. Miner, PhD, received his doctoral degree from St. Louis University. He is Assistant Professor of Family Practice and Community Health and heads the sex offender treatment program at the University of Minnesota's Program in Human Sexuality. Dr. Miner is Vice President of the International Association for the Treatment of Sexual Offenders and past editor of the *Forum,* the newsletter for the Association for the Treatment of Sexual Abusers. He has been the editor, along with Dr. Eli Coleman, of a previous special issue of the *Journal of Psychology & Human Sexuality*, entitled *Sexual Offender Treatment: Biopsychosocial Perspectives*, and was also guest editor for a special issue of *Sexual Abuse: A Journal of Research and Treatment,* entitled *Treatment Outcome Research*. Dr. Miner has published numerous articles and book chapters on sex offender treatment, forensic assessment, instrument development, and evaluation methodology. His current research focuses on understanding the factors that lead to sexual interest in children. The U.S. Department of Justice, the U.S. National Institutes of Health, and the Minnesota Department of Corrections have funded Dr. Miner's research.

Eli Coleman, PhD, received his doctoral degree in psychology from the University of Minnesota in 1978. Currently, he is Director of the Program in Human Sexuality, Department of Family Practice and Community Health, University of Minnesota Medical School in Minneapolis, Minnesota (USA). He is the author of numerous articles and books on the topics of sexual orientation, compulsive sexual behavior, sexual offenders, gender dysphoria, chemical dependency and family intimacy and the psychological and pharmacological treatment of a variety of sexual dysfunctions and disorders. He is particularly noted for his research on pharmacotherapy in the treatment of compulsive sexual behavior and paraphilias. Professor Coleman is the founding and current editor of the *Journal of Psychology & Human Sexuality* and the *International Journal of Transgenderism*. Professor Coleman is one of the past-presidents of the Society for the Scientific Study of Sexuality, the past-president of the World Association for Sexology, and President of the Harry Benjamin International Gender Dysphoria Association. He has been the recipient of numerous awards, including the Surgeon General's Exemplary Service Award for outstanding support of the United States Surgeon General as a contributing Senior Scientist on "Surgeon General's Call to Action to Promote Sexual Health and Responsible Sexual Behavior," released June 28, 2001. He has also received the Richard J. Cross Award for Sexuality Education from the Robert Wood Johnson Medical School. He was given the Distinguished Scientific Achievement Award from the Society for the Scientific Study of Sexuality in 2001 and, in June 2002, was awarded the Alfred E. Kinsey Award for outstanding contributions to the field of sexology by the Midcontinent Region of the Society for the Scientific Study of Sexuality.

Introduction:
Sex Offender Treatment:
Accomplishments, Challenges,
and Future Directions

Michael H. Miner, PhD
Eli Coleman, PhD

This edited volume includes selected papers from the 6th International Conference on the Treatment of Sexual Offenders, which convened in Toronto in May 2000. The conference was sponsored by the International Association for the Treatment of Sexual Offenders (IATSO) and the Program in Human Sexuality at the University of Minnesota Medical School. This conference brought together treatment providers, researchers, and supervision personnel from around the world. This volume is part of a series of works which have emanated from the first 6 International Conferences on the Treatment of Sexual Offenders (Coleman, Dwyer, & Pallone, 1992; Coleman & Dwyer, 1996; Coleman & Miner, 2000).

The IATSO was founded during the 5th International Conference on the Treatment of Sexual Offenders that was held in conjunction with

Michael H. Miner and Eli Coleman are members of the faculty, Program in Human Sexuality, Department of Family Practice and Community Health, University of Minnesota Medical School.

Dr. Coleman was Program Chair for the 6th International Conference on the Treatment of Sexual Offenders; Dr. Miner was the Scientific Chair for the meeting.

Address correspondence to: Dr. Michael H. Miner, Program in Human Sexuality, 1300 S. 2nd Street, Suite 180, Minneapolis, MN 55454 USA (E-mail: mminer@famprac.umn.edu).

[Haworth co-indexing entry note]: "Introduction: Sex Offender Treatment: Accomplishments, Challenges, and Future Directions." Miner, Michael H., and Eli Coleman. Co-published simultaneously in *Journal of Psychology & Human Sexuality* (The Haworth Press, Inc.) Vol. 13, No. 3/4, 2001, pp. 1-3; and: *Sex Offender Treatment: Accomplishments, Challenges, and Future Directions* (ed: Michael H. Miner, and Eli Coleman) The Haworth Press, Inc., 2001, pp. 1-3. Single or multiple copies of this article are available for a fee from The Haworth Document Delivery Service [1-800-HAWORTH, 9:00 a.m. - 5:00 p.m. (EST). E-mail address: getinfo@haworthpressinc.com].

Violencia 98 in Caracas, Venezuela, March 22-27, 1998. The election of the first officers occurred during the first General Assembly of the Association during the 6th International Conference in Toronto. The IATSO intends to sponsor biennial International Conferences on the Treatment of Sexual Offenders. The next conference is planned for Vienna in 2002. The Association has adopted the IATSO Standards of Care for the Treatment of Adult Sexual Offenders (Coleman, Dwyer, Abel, Berner, Breiling, Eher, Hindman, Langevin, Langfeldt, Miner, Pfäfflin, & Weiss, 2000) and intends to continue to update them consistent with the advances in knowledge of the treatment of sexual offenders. These Standards are considered to be minimal standards that all treatment providers around the world should adhere to and are complementary and supportive of other published standards of care (e.g., The Association for the Treatment of Sexual Abusers, 1997). One of the important goals of the Association is to advocate for humane, dignified, comprehensive, ethical and effective treatment of sexual offenders throughout the world.

In this volume, we highlight three areas of service provision and research that reflect advances during the last decade and needs for the coming one. We begin with a general overview of the accomplishments, challenges and future directions of sexual offender treatment. This is followed by an article by Borduin and Schaeffer who describe multisystemic treatment, a model they propose for use with juvenile sex offenders. In their paper, the authors argue that empirical evidence does not support current models of cognitive-behavioral treatment, and they propose a model that is systemic in nature, and draws on the empirically derived correlates and causes of serious antisocial behavior. Prescott also argues for movement beyond the current models for treatment of juvenile sex offenders, and presents a treatment approach for residential programs which draws on the knowledge derived from research in the areas of behavioral problems of childhood and special education.

In the area of adult justice, Wilson and Prinzo describe a restorative justice approach to sex offender reintegration into the community. In contrast to such legislative interventions as community notification, the "Circles of Support" described by Wilson and Prinzo mobilize community resources to aid the released offender in his adjustment, rather than branding him a danger to the community. Eher and his colleagues provide a study that integrates three prominent ways of categorizing child molesters, while, in her paper, Miccio-Fonseca presents a preliminary study of the physical and mental correlates of organic brain dysfunction. This study proposes a move, that is prominent across behavioral issues, toward exploring Central Nervous System functioning as a causal factor in sexually inappropriate behavior.

Another paper in this special volume is an interesting case report of the use of leuprolide acetate to treat an individual with pedophilia. Nancy Raymond and her colleagues not only illustrate the potential effectiveness of this medication, but point out the importance of recognizing comorbid psychiatric factors in treating sexual offenders. Their paper illustrates the oftentimes need for a complex array of pharmacotherapies as an adjunct to cognitive-behavioral sexual offender treatment.

REFERENCES

Association for the Treatment of Sexual Abusers (1997). *Ethical Standards and Principles for the Management of Sexual Abusers*. Beaverton, Oregon: Author.

Coleman, E. & Miner, M. (Eds.) (2000). *Sexual Offender Treatment: Biopsychosocial Perspectives*. New York: The Haworth Press, Inc.

Coleman, E. & Dwyer, S.M. (Eds.) (1996). *Sex Offender Treatment: Interpersonal Violence, Intrapersonal Conflict, and Biological Dysfunction*. New York: The Haworth Press, Inc.

Coleman, E., Dwyer, S.M., & Pallone, N.J. (Eds.) (1992) *Sex Offender Treatment: Psychological and Medical Approaches*. New York: The Haworth Press, Inc.

Coleman, E., Dwyer, S.M., Abel, G., Berner, W., Breiling, J., Eher, R., Hindman, J., Langevin, R., Langfeldt, T., Miner, M., Pfäfflin, F., & Weiss, P. (2000). Standards of care for the treatment of adult sex offenders. In Coleman, E. & Miner, M. (Eds.) (2000). *Sexual Offender Treatment: Biopsychosocial Perspectives* (pp. 11-17). New York: The Haworth Press, Inc.

Advances in Sex Offender Treatment and Challenges for the Future

Michael H. Miner, PhD
Eli Coleman, PhD

SUMMARY. This paper describes what the authors believe to be the major advances, the areas of debate, and the future direction of sexual offender treatment as we leave the 20th century and enter the new millennium. In the area of sex offender treatment, the modification of relapse prevention for use with sex offenders has had a profound effect on the way that therapy is done. Additionally, the development of the selective serotonin reuptake inhibitors and other pharmacotherapies has moved the field more toward a bio-psycho-social model of etiology and treatment, and focused more attention on co-morbid psychiatric disorders in the treatment of sexual offenders. The late 1990s saw major advances in the development of actuarial prediction tools for recidivism, and a concerning move toward phallometric stimuli with unclear reliability and validity. Additionally, the development of the Abel Screen for Sexual Interest has provided a promising, but as yet unvalidated, alternative to phallometry. The 1990s were also a period of considerable growth in the application of sexual offender treatment to special populations, such as adolescents, the developmentally disabled, women and children. The major challenge for the future is to develop methodologically sound re-

---

Michael H. Miner is Assistant Professor and Coordinator, Sexual Offender Treatment Program at the Program in Human Sexuality, and Eli Coleman is Professor and Director, Program in Human Sexuality, Department of Family Practice and Community Health, University of Minnesota Medical School.

Address correspondence to: Dr. Michael H. Miner, Program in Human Sexuality, 1300 S. 2nd Street, Suite 180, Minneapolis, MN 55454 USA (E-mail: mminer@famprac.umn.edu).

[Haworth co-indexing entry note]: "Advances in Sex Offender Treatment and Challenges for the Future." Miner, Michael H., and Eli Coleman. Co-published simultaneously in *Journal of Psychology & Human Sexuality* (The Haworth Press, Inc.) Vol. 13, No. 3/4, 2001, pp. 5-24; and: *Sex Offender Treatment: Accomplishments, Challenges, and Future Directions* (ed: Michael H. Miner, and Eli Coleman) The Haworth Press, Inc., 2001, pp. 5-24. Single or multiple copies of this article are available for a fee from The Haworth Document Delivery Service [1-800-HAWORTH, 9:00 a.m. - 5:00 p.m. (EST). E-mail address: getinfo@ haworthpressinc.com].

5

search on which to base our decisions about the treatments to apply, the unique needs of special populations, and the assessment of dangerousness. *[Article copies available for a fee from The Haworth Document Delivery Service: 1-800-HAWORTH. E-mail address: <getinfo@haworthpressinc.com> Website: <http://www.HaworthPress.com> © 2001 by The Haworth Press, Inc. All rights reserved.]*

KEYWORDS. Sexual offender treatment, SSRIs, assessment, risk, phallometry, reoffending, relapse prevention

The publication of the Furby, Weinrott and Blackshaw (1989) review in *Psychological Bulletin* began a debate about the effectiveness of sexual offender treatment that extended well into the 1990s and is still active today. Furby et al. (1989) concluded, after an exhaustive review of the literature at that time, that there was no scientifically valid evidence to suggest that psychotherapeutically-based sexual offender treatment was effective in reducing criminal behavior. This article set the stage for the 1990s, which have been a period of major advances and considerable growth, but also significant stagnation and retrenchment.

This paper will describe what the authors believe are the major advances, the areas of debate, and future directions of sexual offender treatment as we leave the 20th Century and enter into the new millennium. This will not be an exhaustive literature review, nor will we present a meta-analysis. Rather, this paper will highlight the major contributions to our understanding of sexual offender treatment process, procedures, and techniques.

ADVANCES IN SEXUAL OFFENDER TREATMENT

Relapse Prevention

In 1983, two students of Alan Marlatt published a book chapter that described the application of Relapse Prevention (RP) to sexual offender treatment (Pithers, Marques, Gibat, & Marlatt, 1983). This model is based on the assumption that important similarities exist between sexual offending and other "indulgent" behaviors (e.g., substance abuse, overeating, compulsive gambling); specifically, that sexual offending behaviors are defined as leading to a state of immediate gratification, followed by delayed negative consequences (Nelson, Miner, Marques, Russell, & Achterkirchen, 1989). Additionally, RP assumes that there are common behavioral, affective, and cognitive components associated with the relapse process itself (Nelson et al., 1989). This intervention model has been so influential in the field of sexual offender treatment that virtually all treatment programs involve RP or some variant (Laws, Hudson, & Ward, 2000).

In 1984, the State of California (USA) chose to discontinue its state hospital-based sexual offender treatment programs, citing their lack of effectiveness. In so doing, the State Department of Mental Health began a randomly controlled study of the use of RP with incarcerated sexual offenders, the Sex Offender Treatment and Evaluation Project (SOTEP: Marques, Day, Nelson, & Miner, 1989; Miner, Marques, Day, & Nelson, 1990). To date, SOTEP has yet to have the major impact on the field that was expected at its inception. Part of this is likely due to the results of this study, which initially were quite promising (Miner et al., 1990), but have proven to be less impressive with subsequent analyses (Marques, 1999). In the most recent publication of SOTEP findings, there are no significant differences between those who completed the RP-based treatment program and those in the two control groups, non-volunteers and volunteers assigned to no treatment (Marques, 1999), although the trend is toward fewer re-offenses in the treatment group. To date, SOTEP researchers have not published the results of their extensive post-release interviews, which provide outcome measures other than officially reported re-offenses, nor have they published their in-treatment data, other than two very preliminary analyses of re-offense predictors (Marques, Day, Nelson, & West, 1994; Marques, Nelson, West, & Day, 1994). While SOTEP has not had the impact that was expected, the study was just completed in January, 2000. It is likely that the final results of this study will be very informative, if the researchers publish the wealth of data they have accumulated.

As mentioned earlier, the 1990s dawned with skepticism about the effectiveness of sexual offender treatment, at least those interventions based in psychotherapy. Marshall and his colleagues have more recently argued that the accumulating evidence points to the effectiveness of comprehensive cognitive-behavioral programs (Marshall, 1996; Marshall & Barbaree, 1990; Marshall, Jones, Ward, Johnston, & Barbaree, 1991; Marshall & Pithers, 1994). However, Quinsey and his colleagues have argued that the evidence is, at best, sketchy and based on inadequately designed studies (Quinsey, Harris, Rice, & Lalumière, 1993; Quinsey, 1998).

Hall (1995) conducted a meta-analysis on the outcomes studies published after the Furby et al. (1989) review. This study found that there were few studies that met minimal standards for scientific quality, but those identified (n = 12) indicated that cognitive-behavioral and hormonal treatments were effective. In a more recent meta-analysis, Alexander (1999) used more liberal inclusion criteria than Hall (1995), and reached similar conclusions. That is, that "data from multiple studies *suggest that* treatment may lower recidivism rates, at least in some sexual offenders" (p. 112).

So, as we enter the 21st Century, there is still conflict over what evidence is sufficient for determining that interventions for sexual offenders are effective. Some authors argue that without random assignment, our conclusions will always be questionable (Miner, 1997; Quinsey, 1998), while others argue that random assignment is impractical and unethical (Marshall, 1993; Marshall & Anderson, 2000; Marshall et al., 1991; Marshall & Pithers, 1994). So, in the year 2002, we are still challenged to develop practical, scientifically valid studies that will advance our understanding of effective treatment. This, we believe, requires a recasting of the question from "is sexual offender treatment effective?" to "which components of sexual offender treatment are effective, with which populations, delivered by which modalities?" (Marques, 1999; Miner, 1997).

Pharmacological Agents

The 1990s saw an increase in the focus on psychopharmacology in treatment of sexual offenders–in particular the use of selective serotonin reuptake inhibitors (SSRIs) and LHRH agonists. In general, early pharmacological intervention focused on the use of antiandrogens (mydroxyprogesterone acetate (MPA) and cyproterone acetate (CPA) which reduce plasma testosterone, thus resulting in decreased erections and ejaculation, reduced spermatogenesis, and sexual fantasies, along with a general reduction in sexual interest (Bradford, 1983, 1985). The research on the effectiveness of these agents has generally been limited to case studies and single group designs. There have been very few placebo-controlled designs (e.g., Cooper, 1981; Bradford & Pawlak, 1993). These studies have indicated that treatment with antiandrogens does decrease subjective reports of sexual arousal and sexual interests, as well as leading to a decrease in the frequency of sexual behavior. However, while the research indicates that taking antiandrogens decreases re-offending to almost zero, the drop-out rate is extremely high and re-offense rates have been found to exceed 65% of those who discontinue antiandrogen treatment (Grossman, Martis, & Fichtner, 1999).

In the 1990s, the search for more palliative and effective pharmacotherapies increased. Some clinicians turned to the use of leuprolide acetate–a synthetic analog of luteinizing hormone-releasing hormone (LHRH) which is one of the gonadotropin-releasing hormones (GnRH) (Dickey, 1992; Thibaut, Cordier, & Kuhn, 1993, 1996; Cooper & Cernovsky, 1994). Leuprolide acetate initially stimulates the release of production of testosterone and other testicular steroids but with chronic administration testicular steroidogenesis is suppressed. Thus, androgen production is suppressed and this medication functions similarly to other antiandrogens and reduces sexual fantasies and drive. The advantage of leuprolide acetate is that it works at a higher level of the hypothalamic pituitary axis and, as a result, has a lower side effect profile compared to medroxyprogesterone acetate or cyproterone acetate. The antiandrogenic effects are equal to MPA and in some cases has been used effectively when MPA and CPA have failed (e.g., Dickey, 1992). As a result, there has been initial enthusiasm and some clinicians are now favoring this antiandrogenic approach over the traditional MPA and CPA. Or certainly, they are turning to leuprolide acetate when antiandrogens have failed. Obviously, more systematic study of the effectiveness of leuprolide acetate is necessary.

During the 1990s, there has been much more interest in other pharmacotherapies beyond the use of antiandrogens. In particular, there has been a great deal of interest in the use of the newer antidepressant selective serotonin reuptake inhibitors (SSRIs) in the treatment of sexual offenders. The use of such agents is based on the pharmacological action of such agents and on case reports, which have indicated decreased paraphilic fantasies and urges (Coleman, 1991; Bradford, 1997). It has not been clear whether these medications have been effective because of their known sexual side effects or the improved control of anxiety, obsessionality, and depression. It has been speculated that paraphilias may be best understood as part of obsessive-compulsive spectrum disorders (Coleman, 1991). There have been a few open trials which have shown positive results for the use of SSRIs (Kafka, 1991; Coleman, Cesnik, Moore, & Dwyer, 1992; Stein, Hollander, Anthony, Schneider, Fallon & Liebowitz, 1992; Kafka, 1994; Kafka & Prentky, 1992; Bradford et al., 1996), but to date there have been no published double-blind, placebo controlled studies.

The use of SSRIs has increased our armamentarium of pharmacotherapies beyond the antiandrogens. They have given us more tools in which to treat sexual offenders. The general advantage of the SSRIs over the antiandrogens has been the ease in administration, lowered side effect profile, and the ability to address other psychiatric comorbidity–especially anxiety and depression which seem to be significant triggers in an offender's offense cycle. In general, today, the SSRIs have replaced the antiandrogens as a first-line treatment of paraphilias. In general, however, our knowledge of the usefulness of pharmacotherapy is similar to that for other forms of intervention. That is, the research has shown some promise, but there has not been sufficient scientific rigor in the studies to draw definitive conclusions. We are obviously in need of more double-blind, placebo-controlled studies analyzing the effectiveness of these medications. The problem seems to be the lack of interest by federal agencies or the pharmaceutical industry to support this type of research. There are also ethical issues that make placebo-controlled studies difficult.

Conclusions

While there have been other advances in our understanding of sexual offenders, and there have been other topics addressed in the research, we believe that the development and application of relapse prevention and the move toward more use of a wider range of psychopharmacologic agents are the two major advances of the last decade. The application of RP has lead to movement away from a strict behavioral conceptualization of sexual offender treatment and has lead to more comprehensive treatment programs. Such issues as empathy, sexual education, social skills, and even the modification of sexual fantasy can be integrated within an RP framework. RP, while ubiquitous in the treatment field, is currently being challenged and expanded (Laws, Hudson, & Ward, 2000). However, it still remains the framework and in many ways the redefinition is taking advantage of the richness of the model itself.

Similarly, the introduction of the SSRIs has lead to a better understanding of the issues involved in sexual offending. The apparent success of the application of these agents has lead to more focus on psychiatric comorbidity (Raymond, Coleman, Ohlerking, Christenson, & Miner, 1999), and has promoted the use of pharmacologic agents which have been found to be effective to treat these comorbid conditions. This has also given treatment providers a wider array of treatment options to help their patients to control their offending behavior.

In all areas, the research has been lacking and inadequate. While some authors argue that random assignment studies are unethical (Marshall & Anderson, 2000), it is clear that more methodologically rigorous studies are necessary, both in the application of cognitive behavioral techniques and the use of SSRIs.

ADVANCES IN ASSESSMENT

Actuarial Risk Assessment

Perhaps the area where the most scientific progress has been made is in the assessment of dangerousness. The 1990s showed a proliferation of actuarial prediction tools for risk assessment for adult sexual offenders. Three parallel, and sometimes intersecting, efforts of research have had the most impact in this movement: Hanson and his colleagues in the Office of the Solicitor General of Canada, Quinsey and his colleagues at the Penetanguishene Mental Health Centre in Ontario, Canada, and Epperson and his colleagues at the Minnesota Department of Corrections.

Hanson and Brussière (1998) found that predictors of recidivism differed depending on the type of criminal behavior of interest (e.g., sexual offenses, violent offenses, and general offenses). For example, nonsexual crimes were associated with factors such as being young (under age 25 years), unmarried, and of minority race, and with antisocial or psychopathic personality disorders. In contrast, sexual re-offending was primarily related to variables of a sexual nature: sexual interest in children, prior sexual offenses, victimization of strangers, extrafamilial and male victims, sexual offending at an early age, and perpetration of different types of sexual crimes. Starting from this meta-analysis, Hanson and his colleagues (Hanson, 1997; Hanson & Thornton, 1999) derived two measures to assess risk. The first, the Rapid Risk Assessment for Sexual Offense Recidivism (RRASOR), began with the seven variables found by Hanson and Brussière (1998) to correlate with sex rearrest at least .10 and further refined these through regression analyses. The RRASOR included four variables: prior sexual offenses, age at release or current age, victim gender (for sexual offenses), and relationship of victim to offender (for sexual offenders). The RRASOR was cross validated in a number of populations and compared with other risk assessment tools (explained later in this section). In a further refinement of predictive instrumentation, Hanson and Thornton (1999) compared two instruments, the RRASOR and an instrument used by Her Majesty's Prison System in Great Britain, the Structured Anchored Clinical Judgment (SACJ: Grubin, 1998). The research indicated that when these two instruments were combined, the resultant instrument (STATIC-99) provided better predictive validity than either instrument alone (Hanson & Thornton, 1999). The STATIC-99 includes 10 variables, the four included in the RRASOR and convictions for non-contact sexual offenses, current and prior non-sexual violent offenses, any stranger victims of a sexual offense, prior criminal sentences, and marital status. This instrument was found to predict sexual recidivism better than the Violence Risk Appraisal Guide and Sex Offender Risk Appraisal Guide, but less well than the Minnesota Sex Offender Screening Tool–Revised (described later in this section).

Quinsey and his colleagues at the Penetanguishene Mental Health Centre in Ontario, Canada, studied the predictors of sexual offender recidivism over a 25-year period with samples of maximum-security psychiatric patients (Quinsey, Harris, Rice, & Cormier, 1998). Their work has resulted in the development of two risk assessment tools, the Violence Risk Appraisal Guide (VRAG: Rice & Harris, 1995), and the Sex Offender Risk Appraisal Guide (SORAG: Rice & Harris, 1997). These tools provide methods for predicting the likelihood of violent re-offending in samples of adult sexual offenders.

A group of researchers at the Minnesota Department of Corrections have also been working on predictors of sexual offender recidivism. Their tool the Minnesota Sex Offender Screening Tool–Revised (MnSOST-R) includes many offense description variables, as well as individual history variables (Epperson, Kaul, Huot, Hesselton, Alexander, & Goldman, 1999). The MnSOST-R, unlike the other risk assessment tools, also includes factors related to treatment outcome and completion.

The major problem with all of the above assessment tools is that they are based on static, or unchanging variables, thus cannot take into account progress that an individual may make in treatment to reduce their risk of re-offending. The MnSOST-R attempts to rectify this situation by including two variables, completion of chemical dependency treatment while incarcerated and completion of sexual offender treatment. While these two variables can influence overall risk assessment, they have minimal influence in mediating the effects of the more static variables, since they account for a decrease in only 3 points, but failure to complete treatment can more dramatically influence predicted risk by increasing one's score by 7 points. Additionally, these variables reflect either completion or failure to complete treatment, they do not reflect the changes made during such treatment.

Hanson and Harris (2000a) studied more dynamic factors that might predict sexual re-offenses by comparing a sample of 208 released offenders who had re-offended with a sample of 201 released offenders who had not been apprehended for a new sexual crime. Data collection included interviewing the community supervision officer assigned to each offender and a review of each offender's probation/parole file. Their study indicates that there are a number of changeable factors that differentiate those who re-offend from those who do not. These include drug use, anger problems, social adjustment such as number of significant influences and general social problems, attitudes such as low remorse, rape or child-molesting supportive beliefs, and sexual entitlement, self-management issues such as seeing self at no risk to recidivate and having access to victims, and indications of poor cooperation with supervision. This study lead the authors to develop the Sex Offender Need Assessment Rating (SONAR: Hanson & Harris, 2000b), which they found to significantly predict risk even after controlling for such accepted risk variables as age, IQ, Static-99 and VRAG scores. To date, there are no replications of Hanson and Harris' work, nor does their study help us to determine how to adjust the accepted actuarial scales in light of the more changeable risk factors. The data they present, however, does appear to indicate that there are dynamic risk factors that should be assessed when determining an offender's risk and that more research is needed to determine what these factors are and how they can be incorporated into a risk decision.

Phallometric Assessment and Abel Screen

The major controversy in phallometric assessment as we enter the new millennium is the use of sexually explicit stimuli. While early writers emphasize the need for such stimuli (Laws & Osborn, 1983; Maletsky, 1991), there has been a movement, at least in the United States, to less explicit material. Laws, in an editorial, expressed some concern about the use of nude child stimuli due to issues of informed consent. He recommended using audio stimuli rather than visual stimuli.

In spite of the concerns over the type of stimuli to use for phallometric assessment, there has been little research addressing the effects of different stimuli. In our own research, we have found that discrimination between child molesters with male victims, child molesters with female victims, and rapists requires both visual and audio stimuli (Miner, West, & Day, 1995). Slides of nude children and adults showed differences between child molesters with male victims and the other two groups; however, the discrimination between child molesters with female victims and rapists required audio descriptions of violence, coercion and rape. This study used the same stimulus sets as earlier studies (Abel, Blanchard, Barlow, & Mavissakalian, 1975; Abel, Blanchard, Becker, & Djenderedjian, 1978; Avery-Clark & Laws, 1984; Laws & Osborn, 1983). Therefore, it does not appear that audio stimuli can be substituted for visual stimuli.

The only well-validated stimulus sets include full-frontal nudity (see Freund & Blanchard, 1989; Harris, Rice, Quinsey, Chaplin, & Earls, 1992; Lalumière & Quinsey, 1993, 1994). However, much of the assessment done in the United States is done using non-nude stimuli. This stimulus set has shown some discriminate validity in a so-far-unpublished study (Byrne, 2001) and has never been subjected to independent replication. Additionally, the clothed stimulus set has not been compared to the nude sets, which form the basis for all of the research on the discriminant and predictive validity of phallometric assessment. Another concern with the stimulus set described in Byrne (2001) is that each exemplar is based on a single presentation of a set of slides and audio description and these exemplars are presented in a fixed order. Thus, it is likely that each data point is unreliable and the assessment is subject to order effects.

Interestingly, these problems have not affected the use of phallometric assessment, nor have the suppliers of stimuli appeared particularly concerned about their products' lack of empirical support. In fact, stimulus sets have been developed for special populations, such as the developmentally disabled, with no indication that such sets are necessary, nor any data to guide the differences between sets for special populations and general use.

Abel, Lawry, Karlstrom, Osborn and Gillespie (1994) report on a screening tool that they describe as using "psychophysiological" data which they do not describe. They do show that this tool has some reasonable discriminate validity. In subsequent writings, Abel does describe his measure, visual reaction time. In further research into the reliability and validity of the use of visual reaction time as a measure of sexual interest, Abel, Huffman, Warberg, and Holland (1998) found good reliability and indications of validity in that visual reaction time showed significant associations with self-reported sexual interest. Unfortunately, Abel et al. (1998) do not provide the correlation coefficients, they only report whether or not the correlations were significant (p. 88-89). Additionally, the statistical adequacy of Abel et al.'s methodology has been questioned by Fischer and Smith (1999). They question the interpretation of ipsative z-scores described in the manuals

(Abel, 1996, 1997) and the manner in which the reliability estimates presented in Abel et al. (1998) were calculated.

Due to the proprietary nature of the Abel instrumentation, there has been little independent replication of the psychometric properties of this methodology. Recently, however, more work has addressed the viewing time measure of sexual preference. Zabarauckas and Laws (2000) reported on a sample of 26 forensic patients that viewing time showed better classification than self-report measures when assessing age preference and gender preference. They did not compare viewing time with phallometric assessment. Unlike the Abel instrumentation, Zabarauckas and Laws (2000) used stimuli including both clothed and nude models. They found that the most accurate classifications were demonstrated by use of both nude and clothed stimuli, and poorest results when only clothed stimuli were used.

In a study of adolescents, Smith and Fischer (1999) explored the test-retest reliability and the validity of visual reaction time in a sample of adolescents. Their analyses indicated poor reliability, as well as poor ability to discriminate between offenders and non-offenders and to categorize offenders with respect to age and gender preference. Abel has questioned the adequacy of this study on a number of grounds (Abel, 2000).

Conclusions

There have been a number of major advances over the last decade in the area of assessment for sexual offenders. The most significant advances have been in the area of actuarial assessment. As we enter the new millennium, we have a number of empirically validated tools to use to assess the re-offense potential of identified sexual offenders. Unfortunately, the current state of risk assessment does not provide empirical direction on how to incorporate treatment effects and individual changes into the prediction made by use of the actuarial measures, which focus on historical and other static variables.

The research appears to indicate that phallometric assessment is an important and very useful procedure for assessment of sexual offenders. However, it appears that the current procedures in use, especially in the United States, are dissimilar enough from those used in the research to call into question the validity of commonly used phallometric assessment. The major issue is the nature of the stimuli used. Currently, there is no evidence that the clothed, single exemplar stimulus set has adequate reliability and validity, and the only study to compare clothed and nude stimuli, which used viewing time, not erectile response, seems to question the discriminate validity of clothed stimuli.

The Abel instrumentation was developed to avoid the issues raised by phallometric assessment. While it appears to have promise, this methodology has just begun to be exposed to independent replication with mixed results. Further, the study by Zabarauckas and Laws (2000) may indicate that even this methodology would be best conducted if nude stimuli were included. Such a change would eliminate one of the major advantages of the Abel instrumentation.

ADOLESCENT SEXUAL OFFENDERS

Since 1983, there has been a proliferation of specialized treatment programs for sexually abusive youth, increasing from 20 in 1983 to more than 800 in 1993 (Freeman-Longo, Bird, Stevensen, & Fiske, 1995). These programs have largely been based on interventions developed for adult offenders, with a strong emphasis on Relapse Prevention (Murphy & Page, 2000). It is currently the consensus of experts in the field of sexual offender intervention that group therapy is the treatment modality of choice with this population (Camp & Thyer, 1993; Ryan, 2000), and virtually all programs treating juvenile sexual offenders rely extensively on group interventions (Safer Society Foundation, 2001; Sapp & Vaughn, 1990). Further, both conditional release programs and corrections-based programs are offense-specific, thus implying that juvenile sexual offenders have specialized treatment needs and differ in important ways from other juvenile delinquents.

However, the research conducted to date has shown few differences between adolescent sexual offenders and other delinquent youth (Awad & Saunders, 1991; Benoit & Kennedy, 1992; Blaske et al., 1989; Fagan & Wexler, 1988; Ford & Linney, 1995; Jacobs et al., 1997; Katz, 1990; Moody et al., 1994; Oliver et al., 1993). Additionally, there has been little consideration of the developmental issues related to adolescents. Both treatment programs and legal sanctions have failed to consider the well-established data indicating that most delinquent youth do not continue criminal behavior into adulthood (Moffitt, 1993). Additionally, there have been few studies that have successfully identified factors that predict which juveniles will progress to adult sexual crimes (Kahn & Chambers, 1991; Prentky, Harris, Frizzell, & Righthand, 2000; Smith & Monastersky, 1986; Rasmussen, 1999; Weinrott, 1996).

The failure to find differences between adolescent sexual offenders and other juvenile delinquents has lead some to question the currently used treatment approaches. In this volume, we have included two articles (Borduin & Schaeffer; Prescott) that present approaches that appear to consider both developmental issues and that discuss the similarities between adolescents who commit sexual crimes and those who act out by engaging in other illegal or problematic behaviors.

CONCLUSIONS AND FUTURE DIRECTIONS

In the decade of the 1990s there have been major changes and advances in the field of sexual offender treatment. The areas presented above reflect what the authors believe are the most influential, both in terms of influencing the provision of treatment and fostering empirical investigation. Relapse prevention has changed the thinking of many in the field of sexual offender treatment. Due to its influence, investigators are looking beyond conditioning theories and social skills, the intervention and research areas that dominated the pre-1990s literature. In addition, there is consensus amongst treatment specialists that cognitive-behavior-based interventions are the interventions of choice, although the empirical evidence for this is still questionable.

In the United States, there has been a movement toward identifying the most dangerous sexual offenders and using civil commitment procedures to indefinitely detain them (Sexual Predator Laws). This process requires well-developed techniques for identifying those most at risk, an area of study that has shown major advances in the last 10 years. At the present time, a number of well-designed and empirically-validated actuarial assessment procedures have been developed. These instruments have much in common, but also have some important differences. To date, there is no empirical evidence that one tool is consistently better than another, nor are there empirically-validated methods for the assessor to use in combining or comparing the results of different tools. The other major gap in our knowledge of risk assessment is how treatment progress and dynamic, or changeable, factors influence offender risk. This gap reflects an important limitation of our ability to predict re-offense risk, in that if treatment is effective, it should lower the risk of re-offense in measurable ways.

An area that the authors find especially disturbing is the movement in the United States away from empirically-validated stimulus sets for phallometric assessment. Political forces have influenced the abandonment of nude stimuli for assessment of age and gender preference. In moving from full frontal nudity to minimally clothed stimuli, there have been no attempts to determine that the newly created, or modified stimuli have the same psychometric properties as the stimuli that have been used in all of the research establishing the usefulness of phallometric assessment. Another change in the landscape has been the development of the Abel Assessment for Sexual Interest. This method uses viewing time measurements, along with self-reported interest. To date, the Abel procedure, while certainly a promising tool, has had minimal independent validation, and thus must be viewed with some skepticism.

The final advance in the last ten years has been the proliferation of sexual offender treatment for special populations. In this paper we reviewed the progress in treatment of juvenile sexual offenders. We limited our review to that population because adolescents have been the best studied special population. As the millennium dawns, there has been considerable growth in the treatment of the developmentally disabled. The authors have identified no empirical investigation of this population, either with respect to treatment effectiveness or the specific treatment needs of this group. It is our belief that this is an area that is in need of considerable attention. The developmentally disabled population provides special challenges to intervention and it is not clear that the cognitive-behavioral interventions currently in use are appropriate.

Sexual offender treatment providers also find themselves with the challenges of treating more women. Again, this is a special population that suffers from the dearth of empirical investigation. Generally, this has been because of the fact that only small numbers of women are identified and thus no one has been able to generate a sufficient sample size for meaningful research.

The last special population has gone by many labels, the most prominent being "sexually-reactive" youth. These are prepubescent children identified as having coerced others sexually. Programs for this population are relatively new and have mainly been based on the interventions used with adolescents. At this point, there is considerable confusion on what type of behavior should lead to intervention. Also, there is no evidence that sexual acting out in this population is influenced by different factors than any other acting out behaviors. Current treatment programs, thus, are basically developing based on assumptions with no empirical guidance. This may lead to as much damage to the development of these children as help.

In short, there has been a great deal of change in the field of sexual offender treatment in the 1990s. We have, over the last 10 years, become a much larger field. We are definitely a multi-disciplinary group that includes professionals from both the mental health and the criminal justice systems. Additionally, we reflect disciplines with varying perspectives on the evidence necessary to make decisions and the process by which certain decisions are made. Sexual offender treatment has made a great deal of progress since the dawning of the 1990s. The challenge for the new millennium is to develop a stronger empirical base to support our interventions, whether they are pharmacological, psychological, or legislative. It is also important to develop programs for special populations that are guided by the scientific literature, and reflect the empirically documented unique needs of these populations.

REFERENCES

Abel, G.G. (1996). *A new objective test for youthful offenders. The Abel assessment for interest in paraphilias.* Atlanta, GA: Abel Screening, Inc.

Abel, G.G. (2000). The importance of meeting research standards: A reply to Fischer and Smith's articles on the Abel Assessment for Sexual Interest. *Sexual Abuse: A Journal of Research and Treatment, 12,* 155-161.

Abel, G.G. (1997). *Abel assessment for sexual interest: Judges' product information.* Atlanta, GA: Abel Screening, Inc.

Abel, G.G., Blanchard, E.B., Barlow, D.H., & Mavissakalian, M. (1975). Identifying specific erotic cues in sexual deviation by audiotaped descriptions. *Journal of Applied Behavior Analysis, 8,* 247-260.

Abel, G.G., Blanchard, E.B., Becker, J.V., & Djenderedjian, A. (1978). Differentiating sexual aggressives with penile measures. *Criminal Justice and Behavior, 5,* 315-332.

Abel, G.G., Lawry, S.S., Karlstrom, E., Osborn, C.A., & Gillespie, C.F. (1994). Screening tests for pedophilia. *Criminal Justice and Behavior, 21,* 115-131.

Abel, G.G., Huffman, J., Warber, B.W., & Holland, C.L. (1998). Visual reaction time and plethysmography as measures of sexual interest in child molesters. *Sexual Abuse: A Journal of Research and Treatment, 10,* 81-85.

Alexander, M.A. (1999). Sexual offender treatment efficacy revisited. *Sexual Abuse: A Journal of Research and Treatment, 11,* 101-116.

Avery-Clark, C.A. & Laws, D.R. (1984). Differential erection response patterns of sexual child abusers to stimuli describing activities with children. *Behavior Therapy, 15,* 71-83.

Awad, G.A. & Saunders, E.B. (1991). Male adolescent sexual assaulters: Clinical observations. *Journal of Interpersonal Violence, 6,* 446-460.

Benoit, J.L. & Kennedy, W.A. (1992). The abuse history of male adolescent sex offenders. *Journal of Interpersonal Violence, 7,* 543-548.

Blaske, D.M., Borduin, C.M., Henggeler, S.W., & Mann, B.J. (1989). Individual, family, and peer characteristics of adolescent sex offenders and assaultive offenders. *Developmental Psychology, 25,* 846-855.

Bradford, J.M.W. (1983). Research on sex offenders. In R.L. Sadoff (Ed.), *The Psychiatric Clinics of North America* (pp. 715-733). Philadelphia: Saunders.

Bradford, J.M.W. (1985). Organic treatments for the male sexual offender. *Behavioral Sciences and the Law, 3*, 355-375.

Bradford, J.M.W. (1997). Medical interventions in sexual deviance. In D.R. Laws & W. O'Donohue (Eds.), *Sexual deviance: Theory, assessment, and treatment* (pp. 449-464). New York: Guilford.

Bradford, J.M.W. & Pawlak, A. (1993). Double-blind crossover study of cyproterone acetate in the treatment of paraphilias. *Archives of Sexual Behavior, 22*, 383-402.

Byrne, P.M. (2001). Reliability and validity of less explicit audio and 'clothed' visual penile plethysmograph stimuli with child molesters and nonoffenders. Unpublished doctoral dissertation, University of Utah, Salt Lake City.

Camp, B.H. & Thyer, B.A. (1993). Treatment of adolescent sex offenders: A review of empirical research. *Journal of Applied Social Sciences, 17*, 191-206.

Coleman, E. (1991). Compulsive sexual behavior: New concepts and treatments. *Journal of Psychology & Human Sexuality, 4*, 37-52.

Coleman, E., Cesnik, J., Moore, A., & Dwyer, S.M. (1992). An exploratory study of the role of psychotropic medications in the treatment of sex offenders. *Journal of Offender Rehabilitation, 18* (3/4), 75-88.

Cooper, A.J. (1981). A placebo-controlled trial of the antiandrogen cyproterone acetate in deviant hypersexuality. *Comprehensive Psychiatry, 22* (5), 458-465.

Cooper, A.J. & Cernovsky, Z.Z. (1994). Comparison of cyproterone acetate (CPA) and leuprolide acetate (LHRH agonist) in a chronic pedophile: A clinical case study. *Social and Biological Psychiatry, 36*, 269-271.

Dickey, R. (1992). The management of a case of treatment-resistant paraphilia with a long-acting LHRH agonist. *Canadian Journal of Psychiatry, 37*, 567-569.

Epperson, D.L., Kaul, J.D., Huot, S.J., Hesselton, D., Alexander, W., & Goldman, R. (1999). *Minnesota Sex Offender Screening Tool Revised (MnSOST-R)*. St. Paul, MN: Minnesota Department of Corrections.

Fagan, J. & Wexler, S. (1988). Explanations of sexual assault among violent delinquents. *Journal of Adolescent Research, 3*, 363-385.

Fischer, L. & Smith, G. (1999). Statistical adequacy of the Abel assessment for interest in paraphilias. *Sexual Abuse: A Journal of Research and Treatment, 11*, 195-205.

Ford, M.E. & Linney, J.A. (1995). Comparative analysis of juvenile sexual offenders, violent nonsexual offenders, and status offenders. *Journal of Interpersonal Violence, 10*, 56-70.

Freeman-Longo, R., Bird, Stevenson, W., & Fiske, J. (1995). *1994 nationwide survey of treatment programs and models*. Brandon, VT: Safer Society Press.

Fruend, K. & Blanchard, R. (1989). Phallometric diagnosis of pedophilia. *Journal of Consulting and Clinical Psychology, 57*, 100-105.

Furby, L., Weinrott, M.R., & Blackshaw, L. (1989). Sex offender recidivism: A review. *Psychological Bulletin, 105*, 3-30.

Grossman, L.S., Martis, B., & Fichtner, C.G. (1999). Are sex offenders treatable? A research review. *Psychiatric Services, 50*, 349-361.

Grubin, D. (1998). *Sex offending against children: Understanding the risk*. Police Research Series Paper 99. London: Home Office.

Hall, G.C.N. (1995). Sexual offender recidivism revisited: A meta-analysis of recent treatment studies. *Journal of Consulting and Clinical Psychology, 63,* 802-809.

Hanson, R.K. (1997). *The development of a brief actuarial risk scale for sexual offense recidivism.* User report 1997-04. Ottawa, Ontario: Department of the Solicitor General of Canada.

Hanson, R.K. & Bussière, M.T. (1998). Predicting relapse: A meta-analysis of sexual offender recidivism studies. *Journal of Consulting and Clinical Psychology, 66,* 348-362.

Hanson, R.K. & Harris, A.J.R. (2000a). Where should we intervene? Dynamic predictors of sexual offense recidivism. *Criminal Justice and Behavior, 27,* 6-35.

Hanson, R.K. & Harris, A. (2000b). *The sex offender needs assessment rating (SONAR): A method for measuring change in risk levels.* User report 2000-1. Ottawa, Ontario: Department of the Solicitor General of Canada.

Hanson, R.K. & Thornton, D. (1999). *Static-99: Improving actuarial risk assessments for sex offenders.* User report 99-02. Ottawa, Ontario: Department of the Solicitor General of Canada.

Harris, G.T., Rice, M.E., Quinsey, V.L., Chaplin, T.C., & Earls, C. (1992). Maximizing the discriminant validity of phallometric assessment data. *Psychological Assessment, 4,* 502-511.

Jacobs, W.L., Kennedy, W.A., & Meyer, J.B. (1997). Juvenile delinquents: A between-group comparison study of sexual and nonsexual offenders. *Sexual Abuse: A Journal of Research and Treatment, 9,* 201-217.

Kafka, M.P. (1991). Successful treatment of paraphilic coercive disorder (a rapist) with fluoxetine hydrochloride. *British Journal of Psychiatry, 158,* 844-847.

Kafka, M.P. (1994). Sertraline pharmacotherapy for paraphilias and paraphilia-related disorders: An open trial. *Annals of Clinical Psychiatry, 6,* 189-195.

Kafka, M.P. & Prentky, R. (1992). Fluoxetine treatment of nonparaphilic sexual addictions and paraphilias in men. *Journal of Clinical Psychiatry, 53,* 351-358.

Kahn, T.J. & Chambers, H.J. (1991). Assessing reoffense risk with juvenile sexual offenders. *Child Welfare, 70,* 333-345.

Katz, R.C. (1990). Psychological adjustment in adolescent child molesters. *Child Abuse and Neglect, 14,* 567-575.

Lalumière, M.L. & Quinsey, V.L. (1993). The sensitivity of phallometric assessment with rapists. *Annals of Sex Research, 6,* 123-138.

Lalumière, M.L. & Quinsey, V.L. (1994). The discriminability of rapists from non-sex offenders using phallometric measures: A meta analysis. *Criminal Justice and Behavior, 21,* 152-175.

Laws, D.R., Hudson, S.M., & Ward, T. (2000). The original model of relapse prevention with sex offenders. In D.R. Laws, S.M. Hudson, & T. Ward (Eds.), *Remaking relapse prevention with sex offenders* (pp. 3-24). Thousand Oaks, CA: Sage.

Laws, D.R. & Osborn, C.A. (1983). How to build and operate a behavioral laboratory to evaluate and treat sexual deviance. In J.G. Greer & I.R. Stuart (Eds.), *The sexual aggressor* (pp. 293-335). New York: Van Nostrand Reinhold.

Maletsky, B.M. (1991). *Treating the sexual offender.* London: Sage.

Marques, J.K. (1999). How to answer the question "Does sexual offender treatment work?" *Journal of Interpersonal Violence, 14,* 437-451.

Marques, J.K., Day, D.M., Nelson, C., & Miner, M.H. (1989). The sex offender treatment and evaluation project: California's relapse prevention program. In D.R. Laws (Ed.), *Relapse prevention with sex offenders* (pp. 247-267). New York: Guilford.

Marques, J.K., Day, D.M., Nelson, C., & West, M.A. (1994). Effects of cognitive-behavioral treatment on sex offender recidivism: Preliminary results of a longitudinal study. *Criminal Justice and Behavior, 21*, 28-54.

Marques, J.K., Nelson, C., West, M.A., & Day, D.M. (1994). The relationship between treatment goals and recidivism among child molesters. *Behavior Research and Therapy, 32*, 577-588.

Marshall, W.L. (1993). The treatment of sex offenders: What does the outcome data tell us? A reply to Quinsey et al. *Journal of Interpersonal Violence, 8*, 524-530.

Marshall, W.L. (1996). Assessment, treatment and theorizing about sex offenders: Developments over the past 20 years and future directions. *Criminal Justice and Behavior, 23*, 162-199.

Marshall, W.L. & Anderson, D. (2000). Do relapse prevention components enhance treatment effectiveness? In D.R. Laws, S.M. Hudson, & T. Ward (Eds.), *Remaking relapse prevention with sex offenders* (pp. 39-55). Thousand Oaks, CA: Sage.

Marshall, W.L. & Barbaree, H.E. (1990). Outcome of comprehensive cognitive-behavioral treatment programs. In W.L. Marshall, D.R. Laws, & H.E. Barbaree (Eds.), *Handbook of sexual assault: Issues, theories and treatment of the offender* (pp. 363-385). New York: Plenum Press.

Marshall, W.L., Jones, R., Ward, T., Johnston, P., & Barbaree, H.E. (1991). Treatment outcome with sex offenders. *Clinical Psychology Review, 11*, 465-485.

Marshall, W.L. & Pithers, W.D. (1994). A reconsideration of treatment outcome with sex offenders. *Criminal Justice and Behavior, 21*, 10-27.

Miner, M.H. (1997). How can we conduct treatment outcome research? *Sexual Abuse: A Journal of Research and Treatment, 9*, 95-110.

Miner, M.H., Marques, J.K., Day, D.M., & Nelson, C. (1990). Impact of relapse prevention in treating sex offenders: Preliminary results. *Annals of Sex Research, 3*, 165-185.

Miner, M.H., West, M.A., & Day, D.M. (1995). Sexual preference for child and aggressive stimuli: Comparison of rapists and child molesters using auditory and visual stimuli. *Behavioral Research and Therapy, 5*, 545-551..

Moffitt, T.E. (1993). Adolescence-limited and life-course-persistent antisocial behavior: A developmental taxonomy. *Psychological Review, 100*, 674-701.

Moody, E.E., Brissie, J., & Kim, J. (1994). Personality and background characteristics of adolescent sexual offenders. *Journal of Addictions and Offender Counseling, 14*, 30-48.

Murphy, W.D. & Page, I.J. (2000). Relapse prevention with adolescent sex offenders. In D.R. Laws, S.M. Hudson, & T. Ward (Eds.), *Remaking relapse prevention with sex offenders* (pp. 353-368). Thousand Oaks, CA: Sage.

Nelson, C., Miner, M., Marques, J., Russell, K., & Achterkirchen, J. (1989). Relapse prevention: A cognitive-behavioral model for treatment of the rapist and child molester. *Journal of Social Work and Human Sexuality, 7*, 125-143.

Oliver, L.L., Hall, G.C.N., & Neuhaus, S.M. (1993). A comparison of the personality and background characteristics of adolescent sex offenders and other adolescent offenders. *Criminal Justice and Behavior, 20*, 359-370.

Pithers, W.D., Marques, J.K., Gibat, C.C., & Marlatt, G.A. (1983). Relapse prevention with sexual aggressives. In J.G. Greer & I.R. Stuart (Eds.), *The sexual aggressor* (pp. 214-239). New York: Van Nostrand Reinhold.

Prentky, R., Harris, B, Frizzell, K, & Righthand, S. (2000). An actuarial procedure for assessing risk with juvenile sex offenders. *Sexual Abuse: A Journal of Research and Treatment, 12*, 71-93.

Quinsey, V.L. (1998). Comment on Marshall's "Monster, victim, or everyman." *Sexual Abuse: A Journal of Research and Treatment, 10*, 65-69.

Quinsey, V.L., Harris, G.T., Rice, M.E., & Lalumière, M.L. (1993). Assessing treatment efficacy in outcome studies of sex offenders. *Journal of Interpersonal Violence, 8*, 512-523.

Quinsey, V.L., Harris, G.T., Rice, M.E., & Cormier, C.A. (1998). *Violent offenders: Appraising and managing risk.* Washington, DC: American Psychological Association.

Rasmussen, L.A. (1999). Factors related to recidivism among juvenile sexual offenders. *Sexual Abuse: A Journal of Research and Treatment, 11*, 69-85.

Raymond, N.C., Coleman, E., Ohlerking, F., Christenson, G.A., & Miner, M. (1999). Psychiatric comorbidity in pedophilic sex offenders. *American Journal of Psychiatry, 156* (5), 786-788.

Rice, M.E. & Harris, G.T. (1995). Violent recidivism: Assessing predictive validity. *Journal of Consulting and Clinical Psychology, 63*, 737-748.

Rice, M.E. & Harris, G.T. (1997). Cross-validation and extension of the Violence Risk Appraisal Guide for child molesters and rapists. *Law and Human Behavior, 21*, 231-241.

Ryan, G. (2000). Treatment of sexually abusive youth: The evolving consensus. *Journal of Interpersonal Violence, 14*, 422-436.

Safer Society Foundation (2001). *2000 Safer Society Foundation nationwide survey of treatment programs and models.* Brandon, VT: Author.

Sapp, A.D. & Vaughn, M.S. (1990). Juvenile sex offender treatment at state-operated correctional institutions. *International Journal of Offender Therapy and Comparative Criminology, 21*, 131-143.

Smith, G. & Fischer, L. (1999). Assessment of juvenile sexual offenders: Reliability and validity of the Abel assessment of interest in paraphilia. *Sexual Abuse: A Journal of Research and Treatment, 11*, 207-216.

Smith, W.R. & Monastersky, C. (1986). Assessing juvenile sexual offenders' risk for reoffending. *Criminal Justice and Behavior, 13*, 115-140.

Stein, D. J., Hollander, E., Anthony, D.T., Schneider, F.R., Fallon, B.A., & Liebowitz, M.R. (1992). Serotoninergic medications for sexual obsessions, sexual addictions and paraphilias. *Journal of Clinical Psychiatry, 53*, 267-271.

Thibaut, F., Cordier, B., & Kuhn, J.M. (1993). Effect of a long-lasting gonadotrophin hormone-releasing hormone agonist in six cases of severe male paraphilia. *Acta Psychiatrica Scandinavia, 87* (6), 445-450.

Thibaut, F., Cordier, B., & Kuhn, J.M. (1996). Gonadotrophin hormone releasing hormone Agonist in cases of severe paraphilia: A lifetime treatment? *Psychoneuroendocrinology, 21*(4), 411-419.

Weinrott, M.R. (1996). *Juvenile sexual aggression: A critical review* (Center Paper 005). Boulder, CO: Center for the Study and Prevention of Violence, Institute of Behavioral Science, University of Colorado.

Wincze, W.P., Bansal, S., & Malamud, M. Effects of medroxyprogesterone acetate on subjective arousal, arousal to erotic stimulation and nocturnal penile tumescence in male sex offenders. *Archives of Sexual Behavior, 15*, 293-305.

Zabarauckas, C.L. & Laws, D.R. (2000, November). Innovations in sex offender assessment using computer-generated stimuli: An assessment package of physiological and self-report measures. Poster presented at the 19th Annual Research and Treatment Conference of the Association for Treatment of Sexual Abusers, San Diego, CA.

Multisystemic Treatment of Juvenile Sexual Offenders: A Progress Report

Charles M. Borduin, PhD
Cindy M. Schaeffer, PhD

SUMMARY. Multisystemic therapy (MST) is an ecologically-based treatment model that has proven effective with violent and chronic juvenile offenders and that holds promise with juvenile sexual offenders. This article describes the empirical underpinnings, theoretical foundation, and clinical features of MST and provides a brief review of MST outcome studies with juvenile sexual offenders. The theoretical foundation and clinical features of MST draw upon empirical findings regarding the multidetermined nature of serious antisocial behavior as well as upon social-ecological models of behavior in which the youth and family's school, work, peers, and neighborhood are viewed as interconnected systems with dynamic and reciprocal influences on the behavior of family members. In two randomized trials with juvenile sexual offenders, MST has had positive effects on key social-ecological factors (e.g., family affective relations, peer relations, school performance) associated with sexual offending and has demonstrated long-term reduc-

Charles M. Borduin and Cindy M. Schaeffer are affiliated with the Department of Psychological Sciences, University of Missouri-Columbia.

Address correspondence to: Dr. Charles M. Borduin, Department of Psychological Sciences, 210 McAlester Hall, University of Missouri, Columbia, MO 65211-2500 (E-mail: BorduinC@missouri.edu).

[Haworth co-indexing entry note]: "Multisystemic Treatment of Juvenile Sexual Offenders: A Progress Report." Borduin, Charles M., and Cindy M. Schaeffer. Co-published simultaneously in *Journal of Psychology & Human Sexuality* (The Haworth Press, Inc.) Vol.13, No. 3/4, 2001, pp. 25-42; and: *Sex Offender Treatment: Accomplishments, Challenges, and Future Directions* (ed: Michael H. Miner, and Eli Coleman) The Haworth Press, Inc., 2001, pp. 25-42. Single or multiple copies of this article are available for a fee from The Haworth Document Delivery Service [1-800-HAWORTH, 9:00 a.m. - 5:00 p.m. (EST). E-mail address: getinfo@haworthpressinc.com].

tions in criminal activity and incarceration. The success of MST can be attributed primarily to (a) the match between MST intervention foci and empirically identified correlates/causes of sexual offending in youths and (b) the flexible use of well-validated intervention strategies in the natural environment. *[Article copies available for a fee from The Haworth Document Delivery Service: 1-800-HAWORTH. E-mail address: <getinfo@ haworthpressinc.com> Website: <http://www.HaworthPress.com> © 2001 by The Haworth Press, Inc. All rights reserved.]*

KEYWORDS. Juvenile sexual offenders, sexual offending, violence, delinquency, multisystemic therapy, treatment outcome

Aggressive and nonaggressive sex offenses committed by juveniles present significant problems at several levels of analysis, and these problems argue for the development of effective treatment approaches. On a personal level, juveniles who commit sexual crimes experience numerous psychosocial problems as well as reduced educational and occupational opportunities (Becker, 1998; Davis & Leitenberg, 1987). Moreover, sexual offenses, whether perpetrated by juveniles or adults, have extremely detrimental emotional, physical, and economic effects on victims, the families of victims and perpetrators, and the larger community (Beitchman et al., 1992; Finkelhor, 1990; Ryan & Lane, 1997). Therefore, effective treatment may not only benefit the juvenile and his or her family, but may also save many persons from victimization.

On an epidemiological level, youths under the age of 18 years account for approximately 17% of all arrests for forcible rape and 18% of arrests for other sexual offenses not including prostitution (Federal Bureau of Investigation, 1997). These arrest statistics are especially disturbing in light of Elliott, Huizinga, and Morse's (1985) finding that the ratio of self-reported sexual offenses to actual arrests for sexual offenses by juveniles is approximately 25:1. In addition, about half of all juvenile sexual offenders have prior histories of nonsexual criminal offending (Awad & Saunders, 1991; Fehrenbach, Smith, Monastersky, & Deisher, 1986; Kahn & Chambers, 1991). Thus, if one purpose of treating juvenile offenders is to decrease crime, then juvenile sexual offenders are a logical target for intervention efforts.

On a social services level, juvenile sexual offenders, especially those who are violent, consume much of the resources of the child mental health, juvenile justice, and special education systems and are over-represented in the "deep end" of these systems (Davis & Leitenberg, 1987; Melton, Lyons, & Spaulding, 1998), with considerable cost to the public treasury and intrusion on family integrity and youth autonomy.

Moreover, juvenile sexual offenders often have continued contact with the mental health and criminal justice systems well into adulthood (Abel, Mittelman, & Becker, 1985; Grossman & Cavanaugh, 1989; Groth, Longo, & McFadin, 1982). Therefore, the development of effective treatments for juvenile sexual offenders may help to free resources to address other important problems of children and their families.

Unfortunately, the development of effective treatments for sexual offending in juveniles has been an extremely difficult task. Indeed, more than a decade ago, Davis and Leitenberg (1987) concluded that the treatment outcome literature on juvenile sex offenders was replete with "popular opinion and clinical impressions" (p. 426) and that there was little support for the effectiveness of any given treatment. More recently, Brown and Kolko (1998) noted that there is still "little information regarding successful approaches" (p. 362) to treating juvenile sexual offenders in spite of a proliferation of specialized programs. Conclusions such as these have led many mental health professionals and policy makers to virtually give up on the possibility of attenuating further sexual offending in those youths who are already perpetrators.

To date, the majority of treatments for juvenile sexual offenders have used individual or group therapy to focus on cognitive and behavioral characteristics of the individual youth. Specifically, these treatments often attempt to:

a. reduce denial and increase accountability;
b. increase empathy for the victim;
c. provide insight into precipitating events;
d. address the youth's own victimization, if appropriate;
e. provide sex education;
f. use conditioning procedures to alter deviant arousal patterns;
g. modify cognitive distortions regarding inappropriate sexual behavior; and
h. develop social skills and anger control. (Brown & Kolko, 1998; Davis & Leitenberg, 1987)

Although these interventions have provided a foundation for addressing individual characteristics of juvenile sexual offenders, they fail to address the natural environments of offending youths in ways that support the development of healthy adaptation and attenuate risks for re-offending.

Multisystemic therapy (MST; Borduin & Henggeler, 1990; Henggeler & Borduin, 1990) is an ecologically-based treatment model that addresses multiple determinants of serious antisocial behavior in youths. MST has received the most empirical support as an effective treatment for violent and chronic criminal behavior in youths (see Borduin, 1994; Levesque, 1996; Melton & Pagliocca, 1992; Tate, Reppucci, & Mulvey, 1995) and is a promising treatment for juvenile sexual offenders. The primary purpose of this article is to present the empirical rationale for the application of MST as well as the features of MST that make it well-suited for treating juveniles who have committed sexual offenses. More specifically, this article begins with a brief review of empirical findings regarding the correlates of sexual offending in juveniles. Next, the theoretical foundation of MST is described, followed by a brief description of the clinical features and guiding principles of MST interventions. Findings from randomized clinical trials that demonstrate the efficacy of MST with juvenile sexual offenders are then summarized. Finally, important aspects of MST that contribute to its success and that distinguish MST from commonly available treatments and service programs for juvenile sexual offenders are discussed.

CORRELATES OF JUVENILE SEXUAL OFFENDING

The vast majority of studies examining the correlates of juvenile sexual offending have included relatively serious methodological limitations. For example, there is almost a complete absence of studies that have used appropriate comparison groups (e.g., nonsexual criminal offenders with similar demographic characteristics); without such control groups, it is difficult to determine whether observed results are linked with sexual offending in particular or with delinquency in general. In addition, most studies have combined subgroups of sexual offenders (e.g., child molesters vs. rapists) into a single group and may have obscured potentially important psychosocial differences between them. Furthermore, the data in many of the extant studies are derived from clinical impressions and unstandardized assessment instruments, and the self-reports of incarcerated youths are often the primary source of information (for a discussion of this issue, see Reppucci & Clingempeel, 1978). Notwithstanding these methodological limitations, the extant findings indicate that multiple characteristics of individual youths and their social systems (family, peers, school) are linked with juvenile sexual offending (Becker, 1998; Henggeler, 1989).

Individual Youth Factors

Juvenile sexual offenders show more internalizing problems than do nonsexually offending delinquent youths or nondelinquent youths (Blaske,

Borduin, Henggeler, & Mann, 1989; Kempton & Forehand, 1992). However, despite clinical lore, there is little evidence that the majority of juvenile sexual offenders have a history of sexual abuse (Becker & Murphy, 1998); in fact, prevalence rates of self-reported abuse histories for sexual-offending youth range from approximately 20% to 50% (Becker, 1988; Kahn & Chambers, 1991; Kaufman, Hilliker, & Daleiden, 1996) and are similar to those for other types of juvenile offenders (Awad & Saunders, 1991). Likewise, juvenile sexual offenders have verbal skills that are similar to those of juvenile nonsexual offenders (Lewis, Shankok, & Pincus, 1981; Tarter, Hegedus, Alterman, & Katz-Garris, 1983). Although there is some evidence that victim blaming is related to higher re-offense rates among juvenile sexual offenders (Kahn & Chambers, 1991), the prevalence of other potential cognitive distortions has not been demonstrated (e.g., Hastings, Anderson, & Hemphill, 1997).

Family Characteristics

Research has indicated that, similar to families of other types of juvenile offenders, families of juvenile sexual offenders evidence lower levels of positive communication and warmth than do families of nondelinquent youths (Bischof, Stith, & Whitney, 1995; Blaske et al., 1989). In addition, consistent with findings for families of juvenile nonsexual offenders, families of juvenile sexual offenders show relatively low rates of parental monitoring (Wieckowski, Hartsoe, Mayer, & Shortz, 1998) and high rates of parent-child and interparental conflict and violence (Awad & Saunders, 1989; Davis & Leitenberg, 1987; Fehrenbach et al., 1986). There is also evidence that parents of juvenile sexual offenders have relatively high rates of substance abuse (Graves, Openshaw, Ascione, & Ericksen, 1996; Johnson, 1989).

Peer Relations

Studies have shown that juvenile sexual offenders are more likely to be socially inept and isolated from same-age peers than are other juvenile offenders or nondelinquent youths (Awad & Saunders, 1989; Blaske et al., 1989; Johnson, 1989). Perhaps as a result of isolation from their own peer group, juvenile sexual offenders often turn to younger peers for relationships that are emotionally safer and easier to control (Awad & Saunders, 1989; Fagan & Wexler, 1988; Fehrenbach et al., 1986). Not surprisingly, isolation from same-age peers and preference for younger peers are more common among juveniles who molest younger children than among juveniles who sexually assault same-age peers or adults (Awad & Saunders, 1991; Graves et al., 1996). Although research has found that juvenile sexual offenders tend to have lower affiliation with deviant peers than do juvenile nonsexual offenders (Blaske et al., 1989; Fagan & Wexler, 1988), more work is needed comparing the peer affiliations of different subgroups of juvenile sexual offenders.

School Factors

Juvenile sexual offending has been linked with academic and behavioral difficulties in school, including low achievement, below expected grade placement (Awad & Saunders, 1989; Fehrenbach et al., 1986; Johnson, 1989), behavior problems (Fehrenbach et al., 1986; Gomes-Schwartz, 1984), suspension, and expulsion (Gomes-Schwartz, 1984). However, direct comparisons of sexually offending and nonsexually offending delinquents (e.g., Awad & Saunders, 1991; Ford & Linney, 1995) suggest that these school-related difficulties are not unique to juvenile sexual offenders.

Theoretical and Clinical Implications

The findings from the correlational literature on juvenile sexual offending are consistent with a social-ecological view of behavior (Bronfenbrenner, 1979) and, for the most part, with findings from the literature on juvenile nonsexual offending. Indeed, across studies and in spite of considerable variation in research methods and measurement (e.g., correlational vs. more sophisticated causal modeling studies), investigators have shown that nonsexual offending is multidetermined by the reciprocal interplay of characteristics of the individual youth and the key social systems (family, peers, school, neighborhood) in which youths are embedded. Table 1 lists the correlates that have consistently emerged in the literature on serious antisocial behavior (i.e., nonsexual offending), whether the examined antisocial behavior is conduct disorder (Kazdin, 1995; McMahon & Estes, 1997) or criminal activity (Borduin & Schaeffer, 1998; Thornberry, Huizinga, & Loeber, 1995).

Although the correlates of juvenile sexual offending differ somewhat from those observed for nonsexual offending, the findings from the correlational literature suggest that juvenile sexual offending is multidetermined and that treatment approaches must have the flexibility to address the known correlates of such offending. We believe that the major limitation of individually oriented treatments is that they address

TABLE 1. Correlates of Serious Antisocial Behavior

Individual Youth Characteristics
- Cognitive bias to attribute hostile intentions to others
- Favorable attitudes toward antisocial behavior
- Low verbal skills
- Psychiatric symptomatology

Family Characteristics
- Lax and ineffective parental discipline
- Poor parental monitoring
- Low affection and cohesion
- High conflict and hostility
- Parental difficulties such as drug abuse, psychiatric conditions, and criminality

Peer Relations
- Poor social skills
- Association with deviant peers
- Low association with prosocial peers

School Factors
- Poor academic performance
- Low commitment to education
- Dropout
- Poor academic quality and weak structure of school

Neighborhood and Community Characteristics
- Low social support available from church, neighbors, and the like
- Low organizational participation among residents
- Criminal subculture (e.g., drug dealing, prostitution)
- High mobility

---

only a limited subset of relevant factors in the youth's social ecology, and that effective treatments must have the capacity to intervene comprehensively, at individual, family, peer, school, and possibly even neighborhood levels.

TREATMENT THEORY, CLINICAL FEATURES, AND PRINCIPLES OF MST

The theoretical foundation of MST draws upon the identified correlates/causes of serious antisocial behavior and Bronfenbrenner's (1979) social-ecological theory of behavior. Social-ecological theory views the youth and family's school, work, peers, and community as interconnected systems with dynamic and reciprocal influences on the behavior of family members. Problem behavior can be maintained by problematic transactions within and/or between any one or combination of these systems. Thus, consistent with both the empirically established correlates/causes of youths' criminality and with social-ecological theory, MST interventions target identified youth and family problems within and between the multiple systems in which family members are embedded, and such interventions are delivered in the natural environment (home, school, neighborhood) to optimize ecological validity.

The overriding goals of MST are to empower parents with the skills and resources needed to independently address the inevitable difficulties that arise in raising adolescents and to empower adolescents to cope with familial and extrafamilial problems. Using well-validated treatment strategies derived from strategic family therapy, structural family therapy, behavioral parent training, and cognitive-behavioral therapy, MST directly addresses intrapersonal (e.g., cognitive), familial, and extrafamilial (i.e., peer, school, neighborhood) factors that are known to be linked with youths' serious antisocial behavior, including sexual offending. Biological contributors to identified problems (e.g., major depression, attention deficit hyperactivity disorder) in family members are also identified, and, when appropriate, psychopharmacological treatment is integrated with psychosocial treatment. Because different contributing factors are relevant for different youths and families, MST interventions are individualized and highly flexible.

Although the exact nature and sequence of interventions in MST can vary widely from family to family, several types of interventions are commonly used with juvenile sexual offenders and their parents. *At the family level*, MST interventions generally aim to remove barriers to effective parenting (e.g., parental drug abuse, parental psychopathology, low social support, high stress, marital conflict), to enhance parenting knowledge, and to promote affection and communication among family members; often, conjoint work with family members and other appropriate persons in the offender's social ecology is needed to develop a plan for risk reduction, relapse prevention, and victim safety. *At the peer level*, interventions frequently target youth social skill and problem-solving deficits in order to promote the development of friendships and peer dating; in other cases, interventions are designed to decrease affiliation with delinquent and drug using peers and to increase affiliation with prosocial peers (e.g., through church youth groups, organized athletics, after-school activities). Peer relations interventions are optimally conducted by the youth's parents, with the guidance of the therapist, and often consist of active support and encouragement of relationship skills and associations with nonproblem peers (e.g., providing transportation, increased privileges), as well as substantive discouragement of associations with deviant peers (e.g., applying significant sanctions). Likewise, under the guidance of the therapist, the parents often develop strategies to monitor and promote the youth's *school performance and/or vocational functioning*; interventions in this domain typically focus on establishing positive communication lines between parents and teachers and on restructuring after-school hours to promote academic efforts. Finally, in some cases, *individual interventions* are used with a youth or parent to modify the individual's social perspective-taking skills, belief system, or attitudes that contribute to offending and the sexual assault cycle; intrafamilial victims of the offender may also receive individual treatment for difficulties related to the sexual assault, although the parent or caregiver is reinforced as the change agent and is directly involved with the intervention.

MST is usually delivered by a master's level therapist with a caseload of four to eight families. The MST therapist is a generalist who directly provides most mental health services and coordinates access to other important services (e.g., medical, educational, recreational), always monitoring quality control. Although the therapist is available to the family 24 hours a day, 7 days a week, therapeutic intensity is titrated to clinical need; thus, the range of direct contact hours per family can vary considerably. In general, therapists spend more time with families in the initial weeks of therapy (daily, if indicated) and gradually taper off (as infrequently as once a week) during a 4- to 6-month course of treatment. Treatment fidelity is maintained by weekly group supervision meetings involving three to four therapists and a doctoral level clinical supervisor (usually a child psychologist or child psychiatrist). During these meetings, the treatment team (i.e., therapists, supervisor, and, as needed, a consulting psychiatrist) reviews the goals and progress of each case to ensure the multisystemic focus of therapists' intervention strategies and to identify obstacles to success. Importantly, the team accepts responsibility for engaging families in treatment and for effecting therapeutic change. Thus, when obstacles to successful engagement or to therapeutic change are identified, the team develops strategies to address those obstacles and to promote success.

The nine treatment principles enumerated as follows serve as general guidelines for designing multisystemic interventions. Detailed descriptions of these principles, and examples that illustrate the translation of these principles into specific intervention strategies, are provided in a clinical volume (Henggeler & Borduin, 1990) and a treatment manual (Henggeler, Schoenwald, Borduin, Rowland, & Cunningham, 1998). The reader is referred to these sources for elaboration of the MST treatment model.

1. The primary purpose of assessment is to understand the "fit" between the identified problems and their broader systemic context.
2. Therapeutic contacts emphasize the positive and use systemic strengths as levers for change.
3. Interventions are designed to promote responsible behavior and decrease irresponsible behavior among family members.
4. Interventions are present focused and action oriented, targeting specific and well-defined problems.
5. Interventions target sequences of behavior within and between multiple systems that maintain the identified problems.
6. Interventions are developmentally appropriate and fit the developmental needs of the youth.
7. Interventions are designed to require daily or weekly effort by family members.
8. Intervention effectiveness is evaluated continuously from multiple perspectives with providers assuming accountability for overcoming barriers to successful outcomes.
9. Interventions are designed to promote treatment generalization and long-term maintenance of therapeutic change by empowering caregivers to address family members' needs across multiple systemic contexts.

EFFECTIVENESS OF MST WITH JUVENILE SEXUAL OFFENDERS

Clearly, for both ethical and pragmatic reasons, it is important that mental health services for sexual and other serious juvenile offenders and their families be evaluated rigorously. Rigorous evaluation of outcomes produced by MST has been a high priority since the initial development of this treatment model in the late 1970s. Here, we provide a brief description of MST outcomes with violent and chronic juvenile offenders, followed by a more detailed description of outcomes with juvenile sexual offenders.

Clinical Trials with Violent and Chronic Juvenile Offenders

In an initial outcome study conducted with inner city juvenile offenders (Henggeler et al., 1986), MST was more effective than usual services in addressing key correlates of serious juvenile offending (i.e., decreased youth behavior problems, decreased youth association with deviant peers, and improved family relations). In a subsequent series of studies (Henggeler, Melton, & Smith, 1992; Henggeler, Melton, Smith, Schoenwald, & Hanley, 1993), the effectiveness of MST in treating serious juvenile offenders was established with regard to key measures of criminality (e.g., rearrests, self-reported delinquency, and time incarcerated), as well as with regard to cost savings, at 1-year and 2-year follow-ups. Similarly, Borduin et al. (1995; see also Mann, Borduin, Henggeler, & Blaske, 1990) demonstrated the relative impact of MST on family relations and on parent and youth adjustment in the treatment of chronic juvenile offenders; moreover, substantial between-groups differences in criminal behavior and violent offenses were demonstrated at a 4-year follow-up. Research has also demonstrated that MST leads to lower rates of substance-related arrests in serious juvenile offenders (Henggeler et al., 1991) and to lower rates of reported drug use and fewer days in out-of-home placement (Henggeler, Pickrel, & Brondino, 1999), at substantial cost savings (Schoenwald, Ward, Henggeler, Pickrel, & Patel, 1996), in substance abusing/dependent juvenile offenders.

Clinical Trials with Juvenile Sexual Offenders

Though modest in scope and size ($N = 16$), Borduin, Henggeler, Blaske, and Stein (1990) was the first published randomized trial with juvenile sexual offenders. Youths and their families were randomly assigned to treatment conditions: home-based MST delivered by doctoral students in clinical psychology versus outpatient individual therapy (i.e., an eclectic blend of psychodynamic, humanistic, and behavioral approaches) delivered by community-based mental health professionals. Recidivism results at a 3-year follow-up are revealing. Significantly fewer youths in the MST condition were rearrested for sexual crimes (12.5% vs. 75.0%), and the mean frequency of sexual rearrests was considerably lower in the MST condition (0.12 vs. 1.62). Furthermore, the mean frequency of rearrests for nonsexual crimes was lower for the youths who received MST (0.62) than for counterparts who received outpatient therapy (2.25). The favorable effects of MST supported the viability of conducting a second evaluation of MST with juvenile sexual offenders.

In a recently completed clinical trial, Borduin, Schaeffer, and Heiblum (2000) used a multiagent, multimethod assessment battery to evaluate instrumental (i.e., theory driven) and ultimate (i.e., common to all treatments of juvenile sexual offenders) outcomes in aggressive (i.e., sexual assault, rape) and nonaggressive (i.e., molestation of younger children) juvenile sexual offenders ($N = 48$) who were randomly assigned to MST or usual services. Compared to youths who received usual services, youths who received MST showed improvements on a range of instrumental outcomes, including fewer behavior problems, less criminal offending (self-reported), improved peer relations (i.e., more emotional bonding with peers, less involvement with deviant peers), improved family relations (i.e., more warmth, less conflict), and better grades in school, and their parents showed decreased symptomatology. In addition, youths in the MST condition spent an average of 75 fewer days in out-of-home (i.e., Division of Youth Services) placements during the first year following referral to treatment than did youths in the usual services condition (see Figure 1). Most importantly, an 8-year follow-up of ultimate outcomes revealed that youths who participated in MST were less likely than their usual services counterparts to be arrested for sexual (12.5% vs. 41.7%) and nonsexual (29.2% vs. 62.5%) crimes (see Table 2 for a breakdown of recidivism rates for aggressive and nonaggressive offenders) and spent one-third as many days incarcerated as adults.

Proposed Bases of MST Effectiveness

The results from these outcome studies suggest that MST is a promising approach to the treatment of juvenile sexual offenders. The success of MST, especially in comparison to results from other treatment approaches, is attributed primarily to

    a. the match between MST intervention foci and empirically identified correlates/causes of sexual and other serious juvenile offending (e.g., low family warmth, social immaturity, academic difficulties) and

    b. the flexible use of well-validated intervention strategies in the natural environment.

That is, MST is effective because it directly addresses the multiple determinants of sexual offending in youths' naturally occurring systems. Treatments that address only a small subset of the factors (i.e., individual, family, peer, school) related to sexual offending or that minimize the ecological validity of interventions (e.g., office-based or institution-based treatment) are almost certain to be ineffective in a substantial number of cases (see Henggeler & Borduin, 1995).

FIGURE 1. Time in Out-of-Home Placements One Year After Referral

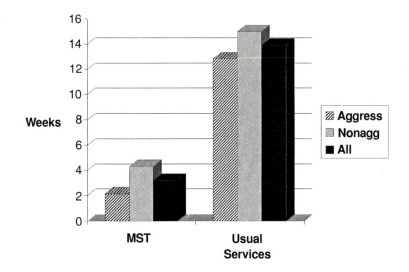

IMPLICATIONS FOR THE DEVELOPMENT OF EFFECTIVE INTERVENTIONS WITH JUVENILE SEXUAL OFFENDERS

The effectiveness of MST in reducing criminality in juvenile sexual offenders has important implications that can help guide the development of potentially more effective interventions for such youths. If, as suggested earlier, a major shortcoming of most treatments for juvenile sexual offending has been their neglect of the multiple correlates of such offending, then the success of MST may be linked with its comprehensive and flexible nature; that is, the results of MST may be due to its explicit focus on ameliorating key social-ecological factors associated with sexual and other criminal offending in juveniles, including behavior problems, parental disturbance, problematic family relations, peer relations difficulties, and poor school performance. In light of the multidetermined nature of sexual (and nonsexual) offending, it is unrealistic to expect even the best conceived office-based treatments to be effective due to their relatively narrow focus.

TABLE 2. Recidivism Rates for Aggressive and Nonaggressive Sexual Offenders by Treatment Group

Recidivism Rate	Treatment Group			
	MST		US	
	Aggressive	Nonaggressive	Aggressive	Nonaggressive
Sexual offenses (%)	16.7	8.3	58.3	25.0
Nonsexual offenses (%)	33.3	25.0	75.0	50.0
Any offenses (%)	33.3	25.0	83.3	58.3

Note. MST = multisystemic therapy; US = usual services.

A second implication of findings from our randomized clinical trials pertains to the accessibility and ecological validity of services. Traditionally, as Melton and Pagliocca (1992) emphasized, mental health services for serious juvenile offenders either have been inaccessible (i.e., office based) or have provided interventions (e.g., residential treatment centers, wilderness programs, incarceration) that have little bearing on the real-world environmental conditions that led to the youth's criminal behavior and to which the youth will eventually return. In contrast, MST is provided in natural community contexts (e.g., home, school, recreation center), with an emphasis on community safety. The delivery of services in youths' natural environments enhances family cooperation, permits more accurate assessment of identified problems and of intervention results, and promotes long-term maintenance of therapeutic changes (Henggeler & Borduin, 1990). Likewise, other aspects of MST (e.g., high levels of accountability for engaging families and achieving outcomes, intensity of training and extensive quality assurance protocols) may also contribute to the positive clinical outcomes that have been obtained with many youths and their families (see Henggeler et al., 1998; Schoenwald & Henggeler, 2002).

In conclusion, our work indicates that a comprehensive intervention, addressing the multiple determinants of antisocial behavior in youths' naturally occurring systems, can successfully reduce criminal activity and incarceration in juvenile sexual offenders. Of course, continued validation and replication are needed for even the most promising treatment approaches. An evaluation of MST that examines mechanisms of change within subgroups of sexual offenders and that provides a more comprehensive follow-up for outcomes and costs is in its beginning stages. The findings of this and other evaluations will ultimately determine whether MST is disseminated as a model for treating juvenile sexual offenders. Nevertheless, given the significant problems that juvenile sexual offenders present for our society, as well as the questionable ethics of providing these youths with treatments that do not produce durable changes, we believe that priority should be placed on the evaluation of promising treatment models such as MST.

REFERENCES

Abel, G., Mittelman, M., & Becker, J. V. (1985). Sex offenders: Results of assessment and recommendations for treatment. *Clinical Criminology: Current Concepts*, 191-205.

Awad, G. A., & Saunders, E. B. (1989). Adolescent child molesters: Clinical observations. *Child Psychiatry and Human Development, 19*, 195-206.

Awad, G. A., & Saunders, E. B. (1991). Male adolescent sexual assaulters: Clinical observations. *Journal of Interpersonal Violence, 6*, 446-460.

Becker, J. V. (1988). Effects of child sexual abuse on adolescent sexual offenders. In G. E. Wyatt & G. J. Powell (Eds.), *Lasting effects of child sexual abuse* (pp. 193-207). Newbury Park, CA: Sage.

Becker, J. V. (1998). What we know about the characteristics and treatment of adolescents who have committed sexual offenses. *Child Maltreatment, 3*, 317-329.

Becker, J. V., & Murphy, W. D. (1998). What we know and do not know about assessing and treating sex offenders. *Psychology, Public Policy, and Law, 4*, 116-137.

Beitchman, J. H., Zucker, K. J., Hood, J. E., DaCosta, G. A., Akman, D., & Cassavia, E. (1992). A review of the long-term effects of child sexual abuse. *Child Abuse and Neglect, 16*, 101-118.

Bischof, G. P., Stith, S. M., & Whitney, M. L. (1995). Family environments of adolescent sex offenders and other juvenile delinquents. *Adolescence, 30*, 157-170.

Blaske, D. M., Borduin, C. M., Henggeler, S. W., & Mann, B. J. (1989). Individual, family, and peer characteristics of adolescent sex offenders and assaultive offenders. *Developmental Psychology, 25*, 846-855.

Borduin, C. M. (1994). Innovative models of treatment and service delivery in the juvenile justice system. *Journal of Clinical Child Psychology, 23*(Suppl.), 19-25.

Borduin, C. M., & Henggeler, S. W. (1990). A multisystemic approach to the treatment of serious delinquent behavior. In R. J. McMahon & R. Dev. Peters (Eds.), *Behavior disorders of adolescence: Research, intervention, and policy in clinical and school settings* (pp. 62-80). New York: Plenum.

Borduin, C. M., Henggeler, S. W., Blaske, D. M., & Stein, R. (1990). Multisystemic treatment of adolescent sexual offenders. *International Journal of Offender Therapy and Comparative Criminology, 34*, 105-113.

Borduin, C. M., Mann, B. J., Cone, L. T., Henggeler, S. W., Fucci, B. R., Blaske, D. M., & Williams, R. A. (1995). Multisystemic treatment of serious juvenile offenders: Long-term prevention of criminality and violence. *Journal of Consulting and Clinical Psychology, 63*, 569-578.

Borduin, C. M., & Schaeffer, C. M. (1998). Violent offending in adolescence: Epidemiology, correlates, outcomes, and treatment. In T. P. Gullotta, G. R. Adams, & R. Montemayor (Eds.), *Delinquent violent youth: Theory and interventions* (pp. 144-174). Newbury Park, CA: Sage.

Borduin, C. M., Schaeffer, C. M., & Heiblum, N. (2000). *Multisystemic treatment of aggressive and nonaggressive sexual offending in adolescents: Instrumental and ultimate outcomes.* Manuscript submitted for publication.

Bronfenbrenner, U. (1979). *The ecology of human development: Experiments by nature and design.* Cambridge, MA: Harvard University Press.

Brown, E. J., & Kolko, D. J. (1998). Treatment efficacy and program evaluation with juvenile sexual abusers: A critique with directions for service delivery and research. *Child Maltreatment, 3,* 362-373.

Davis, G. E., & Leitenberg, H. (1987). Adolescent sex offenders. *Psychological Bulletin, 101,* 417-427.

Elliott, D. S., Huizinga, D., & Morse, B. J. (1985). *The dynamics of deviant behavior: A national survey progress report.* Boulder, CO: Behavioral Research Institute.

Fagan, J., & Wexler, S. (1988). Explanations of sexual assault among violent delinquents. *Journal of Adolescent Research, 3,* 363-385.

Federal Bureau of Investigation, U. S. Department of Justice (1997). *Uniform crime reports.* Washington, DC: U.S. Government Printing Office.

Fehrenbach, P. A., Smith, W., Monastersky, C., & Deisher, R. W. (1986). Adolescent sexual offenders: Offender and offense characteristics. *American Journal of Orthopsychiatry, 56,* 225-233.

Finkelhor, D. (1990). Early and long-term effects of child sexual abuse: An update. *Professional Psychology: Research and Practice, 21,* 325-330.

Ford, M. E., & Linney, J. E. (1995). Comparative analysis of juvenile sexual offenders, violent nonsexual offenders, and status offenders. *Journal of Interpersonal Violence, 10,* 56-70.

Gomes-Schwartz, B. (1984). Juvenile sexual offenders. In *Sexually exploited children: Service and research project.* Washington, DC: U.S. Department of Justice.

Graves, R. B., Openshaw, D. K., Ascione, F. R., & Ericksen, S. L. (1996). Demographic and parental characteristics of youthful sexual offenders. *International Journal of Offender Therapy and Comparative Criminology, 40,* 300-317.

Grossman, L. S., & Cavanaugh, J. L. (1989). Do sex offenders minimize psychiatric symptoms? *Journal of Forensic Sciences, 34,* 881-886.

Groth, A. N., Longo, R. E., & McFadin, J. B. (1982). Undetected recidivism among rapists and child molesters. *Crime and Delinquency, 28,* 450-458.

Hastings, T., Anderson, S. J., & Hemphill, P. (1997). Comparisons of daily stress, coping, problem behavior, and cognitive distortions in adolescent sexual offenders and conduct-disordered youth. *Sexual Abuse: A Journal of Research and Treatment, 9,* 29-42.

Henggeler, S. W. (1989). *Delinquency in adolescence.* Newbury Park, CA: Sage.

Henggeler, S. W., & Borduin, C. M. (1990). *Family therapy and beyond: A multisystemic approach to treating the behavior problems of children and adolescents.* Pacific Grove, CA: Brooks/Cole.

Henggeler, S. W., & Borduin, C. M. (1995). Multisystemic treatment of serious juvenile offenders and their families. In I. M. Schwartz & P. AuClaire (Eds.), *Home-based services for troubled children* (pp. 113-130). Lincoln: University of Nebraska Press.

Henggeler, S. W., Borduin, C. M., Melton, G. B., Mann, B. J., Smith, L. A., Hall, J. A., Cone, L., & Fucci, B. R. (1991). Effects of multisystemic therapy on drug use and abuse in serious juvenile offenders: A progress report from two outcome studies. *Family Dynamics of Addiction Quarterly, 1*, 40-51.

Henggeler, S. W., Melton, G. B., & Smith, L. A. (1992). Family preservation using multisystemic therapy: An effective alternative to incarcerating serious juvenile offenders. *Journal of Consulting and Clinical Psychology, 60*, 953-961.

Henggeler, S. W., Melton, G. B., Smith, L. A., Schoenwald, S. K., & Hanley, J. H. (1993). Family preservation using multisystemic treatment: Long-term follow-up to a clinical trial with serious juvenile offenders. *Journal of Child and Family Studies, 2*, 283-293.

Henggeler, S. W., Pickrel, S. G., & Brondino, M. J. (1999). Multisystemic treatment of substance abusing and dependent delinquents: Outcomes, treatment fidelity, and transportability. *Mental Health Services Research, 1*, 171-184.

Henggeler, S. W., Rodick, J. D., Borduin, C. M., Hanson, C. L., Watson, S. M., & Urey, J. R. (1986). Multisystemic treatment of juvenile offenders: Effects on adolescent behavior and family interaction. *Developmental Psychology, 22*, 132-141.

Henggeler, S. W., Schoenwald, S. K., Borduin, C. M., Rowland, M. D., & Cunningham, P. B. (1998). *Multisystemic treatment of antisocial behavior in children and adolescents*. New York: Guilford.

Johnson, T. C. (1989). Female child perpetrators: Children who molest other children. *Child Abuse and Neglect, 13*, 571-585.

Kahn, T. J., & Chambers, H. J. (1991). Assessing reoffense risk with juvenile sexual offenders. *Child Welfare, 70*, 333-345.

Kaufman, K. L., Hilliker, D. R., & Daleiden, E. L. (1996). Subgroup difference in the modus operandi of adolescent sexual offenders. *Child Maltreatment, 1*, 17-24.

Kazdin, A. E. (1995). *Conduct disorders in childhood and adolescence* (2nd ed.). Thousand Oaks, CA: Sage.

Kempton, T., & Forehand, R. (1992). Juvenile sexual offenders: Similar to, or different from, other incarcerated delinquent offenders. *Behavior Research and Therapy, 30*, 533-536.

Levesque, R. J. R. (1996). Is there still a place for violent youth in juvenile justice? *Aggression and Violent Behavior, 1*, 69-79.

Lewis, D. O., Shankok, S. S., & Pincus, J. H. (1981). Juvenile male sexual assaulters: Psychiatric, neurological, psychoeducational, and abuse factors. In D. O. Lewis (Ed.), *Vulnerabilities to delinquency* (pp. 89-105). Jamaica, NY: Spectrum Publications.

Mann, B. J., Borduin, C. M., Henggeler, S. W., & Blaske, D. M. (1990). An investigation of systemic conceptualizations of parent-child coalitions and symptom change. *Journal of Consulting and Clinical Psychology, 58*, 336-344.

McMahon, R. J., & Estes, A. M. (1997). Conduct problems. In E. J. Mash & L. G. Terdal (Eds.), *Assessment of childhood disorders* (pp. 130-193). New York: Guilford.

Melton, G. B., & Pagliocca, P. M. (1992). Treatment in the juvenile justice system: Directions for policy and practice. In J. J. Cocozza (Ed.), *Responding to the mental health needs of youth in the juvenile justice system* (pp. 107-139). Seattle, WA: National Coalition for the Mentally Ill in the Criminal Justice System.

Melton, G. B., Lyons, P. M., & Spaulding, W. J. (1998). *No place to go: The civil commitment of minors.* Lincoln, NE: University of Nebraska Press.

Reppucci, N. D., & Clingempeel, W. G. (1978). Methodological issues in research with correctional populations. *Journal of Consulting and Clinical Psychology, 46,* 727-746.

Ryan, G., & Lane, S. (Eds.). (1997). *Juvenile sexual offending: Causes, consequences, and correction* (Rev. ed.). San Francisco: Jossey-Bass.

Schoenwald, S. K., & Henggeler, S. W. (2002). Services research and family based treatment. In H. Liddle, G. Diamond, R. Levant, J. Bray, & D. Santisteban (Eds.), *Family psychology intervention science.* Washington, DC: American Psychological Association.

Schoenwald, S. K., Ward, D. M., Henggeler, S. W., Pickrel, S. G., & Patel, H. (1996). Multisystemic therapy treatment of substance abusing or dependent adolescent offenders: Costs of reducing incarceration, inpatient, and residential treatment. *Journal of Child and Family Studies, 5,* 431-444.

Tarter, R. E., Hegedus, A. M., Alterman, A. I., & Katz-Garris, L. (1983). Cognitive capacities of juvenile violent, nonviolent, and sexual offenders. *Journal of Nervous and Mental Disease, 171,* 564-567.

Tate, D. C., Reppucci, N. D., & Mulvey, E. P. (1995). Violent juvenile delinquents: Treatment effectiveness and implications for future action. *American Psychologist, 50,* 777-781.

Thornberry, T. P., Huizinga, D., & Loeber, R. (1995). The prevention of serious delinquency and violence: Implications from the program of research on the causes and correlates of delinquency. In J. C. Howell, B. Krisberg, J. D. Hawkins, & J. J. Wilson (Eds.), *A sourcebook: Serious, violent, and chronic juvenile offenders* (pp. 213-237). Newbury Park, CA: Sage.

Wieckowski, E., Hartsoe, P., Mayer, A., & Shortz, J. (1998). Deviant sexual behavior in children and young adolescents: Frequency and patterns. *Sexual Abuse: A Journal of Research and Treatment, 10,* 293-303.

Collaborative Treatment
for Sexual Behavior Problems
in an Adolescent Residential Center

David S. Prescott, LICSW

SUMMARY. Many residential treatment and sex offender programs for adolescents historically have used coercion-based interventions. Treatment programs employing coercive techniques often replicate the same destructive and intrusive behaviors they seek to eliminate. Tension between departments coupled with poor communication and discomfort around sexual behavior issues within the staff of residential treatment centers are more likely to inhibit the progress of the youths they serve.

Collaboration among residential, educational, and clinical components enables staff to work in a direct, genuine, and respectful fashion with students who have histories of sexually abusive behavior. It further assists in maintaining a safe and predictable environment for these students. Finally, it helps students eliminate destructive behaviors by directly and consistently addressing four key areas: sexually abusive

David S. Prescott is a licensed independent clinical social worker, who supervises the treatment of youths with sexual behavior problems at Bennington School, Inc., Bennington, VT.

Address correspondence to: David S. Prescott, Bennington School, P.O. Box 593, Shaftsbury, VT 05262 USA.

This paper would not have been possible without the ideas and support of Joanne Schladale, Lee Gallagher, Fran Moriarty, Jeff LaBonte, and Louise Lloyd Prescott.

A preliminary version of this paper was presented at the 6th International Conference for the Treatment of Sexual Offenders, Toronto, Canada, May 29, 2000.

[Haworth co-indexing entry note]: "Collaborative Treatment for Sexual Behavior Problems in an Adolescent Residential Center." Prescott, David S. Co-published simultaneously in *Journal of Psychology & Human Sexuality* (The Haworth Press, Inc.) Vol. 13, No. 3/4, 2001, pp. 43-58; and: *Sex Offender Treatment: Accomplishments, Challenges, and Future Directions* (ed: Michael H. Miner, and Eli Coleman) The Haworth Press, Inc., 2001, pp. 43-58. Single or multiple copies of this article are available for a fee from The Haworth Document Delivery Service [1-800-HAWORTH, 9:00 a.m. - 5:00 p.m. (EST). E-mail address: getinfo@ haworthpressinc.com].

43

behavior, antisocial attitudes, social/emotional functioning, and overall self-care. It is not the author's intention to hold Bennington School, Inc. up as a model residential treatment program or to criticize other residential facilities. Rather, it is hoped that what is working in Bennington may be helpful to others.

Many who have worked on the front lines of residential treatment with sexually abusive adolescents have received training in elements specific to sexually abusive behavior. The origins of treatment for youth who have sexually abused were noteworthy for their lack of offense-specific interventions (National Adolescent Perpetration Network, 1993). However, a wealth of literature soon emerged addressing the need for assessment and treatment techniques specific to this population (Perry & Orchard, 1992; Barbaree, Marshall, & Hudson, 1993). Much of this literature made assumptions regarding high levels of chronicity (Perry & Orchard, 1992) while other contributions stressed the role of denial and minimization (Barbaree & Cortoni, 1993). As a result, while many issue-specific forms of assessment and treatment were developed, they often did not take into account other developmental needs and issues in the lives of sexually abusive youths (Lane, 1997).

Concurrent with this emerging research was a substantial increase in the number of treatment programs for juvenile sex offenders (National Adolescent Perpetration Network, 1993). In this context, it is not surprising that many treatment programs relied heavily on treatment targeting denial, minimization, and perceived sexual deviance without taking into account other treatment needs of youths. Although a recent literature review of adolescent residential programs (Curwen, 2000) notes a trend away from shame-based approaches, there appears to be less clarity on specific criteria on which to base residential treatment of adolescents who have sexually abused (Curwen, 2000).

Finally, recent research shows that among adult populations, accepting responsibility for abusive behavior in treatment is more likely to result from a warm, genuine, and empathic treatment style (Marshall, Fernandez, & Anderson, 1999). Group therapy participation, similarly, results from encouragement, open questions, and nonconfrontational challenge. The emerging themes of recent trends and research should inspire those at the front lines of residential treatment to reconsider not just basic treatment approaches, but the most minute elements of their interactions with youths. *[Article copies available for a fee from The Haworth Document Delivery Service: 1-800-HAWORTH. E-mail address: <getinfo@ haworthpressinc.com> Website: <http://www.HaworthPress.com> © 2001 by The Haworth Press, Inc. All rights reserved.]*

KEYWORDS. Juvenile sexual offenders, residential treatment, delinquency, sexual offender treatment

IMPLICATIONS OF RECENT TRENDS
IN UNDERSTANDING YOUTH WHO SEXUALLY ABUSE

Studies of adult pedophiles report that close to half report a juvenile onset to their offending (Barbaree & Cortoni, 1993). While juveniles are responsible for 30%-60% of child molestation (Hunter, 1999; Weinrott, 1996), this does not mean that the majority of adolescents who have sexually abused go on to be pedophiles. Other research suggests that a large percentage of juvenile rapists discontinued the behavior by adulthood (Elliott, 1994).

Understanding youth with histories of problem sexual behavior has, by history, been challenging. The development of sexuality in adolescence has been described as fluid and dynamic (Hunter, 1999). There are contextual issues to consider such as family involvement, school, and community issues (Prentky, Harris, Frizzell, & Righthand, 2000). The base rate for re-offense among juvenile sex offenders is less than other forms of recidivism (Alexander, 1999; Worling, 1999; Langstrom & Grann, 2000). Furthermore, like their adult counterparts, youth who have sexually abused are a heterogeneous population ranging from traumatized and reactive children (Ryan & Lane, 1997) to criminally versatile youth for whom sex offending is just one area of emerging social deviance (Forth & Burke, 1998; Frick, 1998). The current research suggests that the latter end of this spectrum may well be in the minority of youth with histories of sexually abusive behavior.

A number of authors have advanced the state of understanding these youth (Barbaree, Marshall, & Hudson, 1993; Ryan & Lane, 1997; Ryan and Associates, 1999). They contend that the origins of sexually abusive behavior occur both within the child's development and in the context where development occurs (home, school, family, and social relationships). Physical and sexual abuse as well as physical and emotional neglect all play significant roles in the origins of sexual offending. Fuente and Wand (in Ryan et al., 1999) have made a strong argument for understanding "therapeutic intervention as mediation of subsequent life experience" in the treatment of sexually abusive youth.

Fortunately, the rate of sexual recidivism in juveniles is relatively low. A recent meta-analysis (Alexander, 1999) of eight studies with over 1,000 juveniles showed a rate of 7.1% across 3 to 5 years. This compared favorably to adult rates of 13% overall for those who completed treatment and 18% who were untreated. Other studies (Borduin et al., 1990; Worling, 1999) have found encouraging decreases in juvenile recidivism following treatment specifically targeting sexual behavior problems. This may not be surprising in light of studies of recidivism among other serious juvenile offender populations (Loeber & Farrington, 1998).

However, recent research among some populations of sexually abusive youth suggests that general recidivism is more likely to occur than sexual recidivism (Alexander, 1999; Worling, 1999; Langstrom & Grann, 2000). This suggests that the prudent residential program may wish to consider treatment strategies that target a wide range of destructive behaviors.

Recently published data (Prentky, Harris, Frizzell, & Righthand, 2000) challenge traditional notions of who is at the greatest risk to re-offend. In their sample, juvenile recidivists were marked more by an antisocial dimension (including caregiver instability, impulsivity, and aggression) than by a sexual interest dimension. In other words, a key element of sexual offenses by youth may be less driven by sexual interest than the willingness to act on it (Prentky, 2000). It has long been known that adolescence is marked by heightened and changing sexual interest and arousal patterns (Hunter, 1999) but what hasn't been understood is what drives a young person to offend and then re-offend after detection. Further, there is a suggestion that many youths are identified as high risk when, in fact, they aren't, and that many future offenders remain undetected (Prentky et al., 2000).

The net result of this literature supports the idea that sexually abusive youth are indeed a heterogeneous population whose treatment needs cross a number of domains, including the interpersonal, affective, antisocial, and sexually deviant. Treatment involving the promotion of social competency, a healthy sense of masculinity, values clarification, and improved awareness of one's actions on others has greater value than treatment focused on only one of these domains. What is needed now is clearer research into those types of juveniles who are at the highest risk for re-offense (early onset pedophilia, psychopathy) in order to tailor treatment more effectively (Hunter, 1999).

Along these lines, Mark Hubble and his colleagues (Hubble, Duncan, & Miller, 1999) have presented evidence of four domains of "what works in therapy." Among these, a full 40% of successful treatment outcome was found to come from outside the therapy. This includes the client's strengths, environment, attitudes, the support of others, and even good luck. How this correlates specifically with successful methods in treating sexually abusive youth is not immediately clear. However, the role of parents and supportive others in promoting healthy change cannot be underestimated.

A recent meta-analysis (Hanson & Bussière, 1996) noted that failure to complete treatment was a risk factor for recidivism in adult populations. Much discussion has resulted from this finding, and it is uncertain how this translates into predicting relapse in sexually abusive youth. However, it suggests an obligation on the part of adults to ensure that juveniles are able to complete treatment once they start. .

In combination, these studies strongly suggest that in the aggregate, juveniles with sexual behavior problems are different from their adult counterparts:

- Their treatment needs are different (Ryan & Lane, 1997; Ryan et al., 1999).
- Their arousal patterns are more fluid (Hunter, 1999).
- They are more dependent on their environment for managing risk factors.
- Treatment should be applicable to a wide range of life domains (Alexander, 1999; Worling, 1999; Langstrom & Grann, 2000).
- Adults have an obligation to understand the individual's responsivity to treatment in order to properly tailor interventions (Andrews & Bonta, 1998).

AN OVERVIEW OF BENNINGTON SCHOOL, INC.

Bennington School, Inc. is a 24-hour year-round residential treatment center that currently serves over 100 students ranging in ages from 10 to 21. Students are referred from school departments, protective services, and the legal system. They often come from complicated and chaotic backgrounds. Intellectual levels can range from mild mental retardation to superior intelligence. Treatment needs call for interventions across a wide spectrum, ranging from self-contained classrooms to pharmacological interventions. Many students require one-to-one staffing for a major portion of their day. All students receive an intensive level of supervision, structure, staff interventions, and access to clinical staff. Awake night staff are available in all dormitories. An average course of placement is 18 months duration.

THE STUDENTS

Bennington School students come from diverse backgrounds. Many students have been exposed to physical and sexual abuse as well as chronic physical and emotional neglect. More often than not, these events have occurred in combination over the course of many years. The students identified with sexual behavior problems often endure a lengthy process of anxiety and discomfort as they seek to establish themselves in their new environment with a sense of safety, predictability, and self-respect. This sometimes appears to be a completely alien experience. Interaction with non-abusive adults can be confusing and threatening. For many students, acclimation to this environment is among their primary accomplishments.

The students have a wide range of diagnoses, including Post-Traumatic Stress Disorder, Pervasive Developmental Disorder, Reactive Attachment Disorder, and Bipolar Disorder. Diagnoses of Conduct Disorder (with various ages of onset) and Attention Deficit Hyperactivity Disorder are particularly frequent. Learning disabilities and developmental delays are also common.

Students with sexual behavior problems are identified in a variety of ways. Many students are placed with a preexisting diagnosis of a sexual disorder. Many students have been adjudicated for sexual offenses. However, most of these students have been engaged in problem sexual behavior that the legal system, for whatever reason, declined to prosecute. Often, a state protective services or child welfare agency has determined that the student has engaged in problem sexual behavior and has asked for intervention. In many cases, the students have admitted to problem behavior and express a desire to prevent relapse. In some cases students deny and later admit these problems.

PRIMARY CHARACTERISTICS OF DAILY LIFE

Contrary to many facilities serving this type of population, Bennington School does not use a point or level system. There is no token economy. Students do not "earn privileges" but obtain informal access to a wider range of activities through prosocial behavior and attitudes. There is an underlying assumption that all students should be provided at all times with the finest and best possible circumstances and activities. It is the intention that the staff and administration should at all times develop a "culture of giving" rather than a culture of "taking away." The goal of this environment is that students may better take responsibility for their daily lives and actions rather than be forced to do so (Jenkins, 1990). As a result, the notion of the program as a safe haven for youth is the stated goal of daily life at all times (see Salter, 1995; Ryan & Lane, 1997, p. 132). In this way, students may explore their identity, develop an orientation towards their own future, and explore their views of the world (Ryan & Lane, 1997).

Another aspect of daily life is that the development of healthy interpersonal relationships is strongly emphasized but not required. Social competency is stressed through participation in activities such as sports and outdoor adventure programming that advocate constructive risk-taking, team building, and the development of self-confidence. However, students are not formally awarded or sanctioned around this participation. It is intended that by inviting youth to participate in interpersonal relationships they can go about this work at their own pace. Further, it releases the youth from the necessity to form relationships at times in their life when they are not ready (Salter, 1995). By removing the anxiety around compelled attachment, the students may more easily find their way into relationships in which they experience genuine competence. This has been found to be beneficial with youth for whom attachments have been toxic and potentially life threatening in the past (Ryan et al., 1999). Unfortunately, the other people in these students' lives who have appeared kind, generous, and empathic have been the very ones who have abused them.

Finally, a calm approach towards limit-setting and other interventions is maintained and advocated throughout the daily life of the program. Staff interventions based on harsh confrontation and coercion risk replicating abusive environments that the student has survived (see Salter, 1995, pp. 175-83). Further, they do not adequately role model healthy or pro-social problem-solving skills. While momentarily effective, harsh confrontation is ultimately shortsighted with respect to the long-term needs of the student. It may be surmised that harsh confrontation better suits the immediate needs of the adult rather than the student. After all, harsh confrontation is easier to administer than supportive guidance, particularly when the adults are tired and frustrated.

To summarize, many of the students at Bennington School, Inc. have been sexually abusive towards others. Upon evaluation, they often appear to have significant needs around their own history of traumatization. Factors contributing to their abusiveness include underdeveloped skills for productive community living. They are in need of a sense of competence, productivity, efficacy, and a sense of themselves as having an orientation towards a successful future. For these and other reasons, the term "sex offender" is rarely (if ever) used. The potential for the development of a shameful sense of one's identity as hopeless and deviant is too great to allow this. Further, there is the concern that youth who have not been specifically convicted of a sexual offense cannot accurately be portrayed with a legal term. While there is always realistic caution around the potential for re-offense, this caution is not served through the use of pejorative terms. With this context and mission, an approach to treatment based on honor and collaboration is possible.

COLLABORATION

Collaborative treatment with youth with sexual behavior problems requires strength, creativity, and optimism on the part of the adults who implement it. It entails taking a long view of treatment progress and using therapeutic engagement across departments to invite student participation. The following are some elements of this approach which have been successful at Bennington School, Inc.

Departments are of equal value. It is obvious that a chain of command within departments must exist to properly implement the mission of the program. However, a classic problem in residential treatment is the imbalance of power between the residential, educational, and clinical components of the program. Boundaries between the departments can become blurred, staff can become confused around their roles, line staff can become tempted to over-counsel, clinicians can become fierce limit-setters and subvert their own work, etc. A primary concern is the effect of having clinicians become over-valued or viewed as more powerful than other line staff. The results are myriad, include staff perceptions of powerlessness, a poor emphasis on the management of daily routines and obligations, and the belief that all therapy occurs in the therapist's office. The risk for staff and clinical burnout becomes more imminent, and a staff-centered culture of personality replaces a student-centered culture of growth. As a result, a fundamental balance of power among all departments is stressed and reinforced at all times. All staff are viewed as staff first and as members of their departments second. This is the platform for a treatment approach that honors the importance of education, physical health, routines, and relationships as well as the hours of therapy.

Therapeutic engagement. With these egalitarian safeguards in place, a primary focus on self-care, productivity, competence and self-efficacy is then possible. This is accomplished through the promotion of healthy activities and invitations to participate in diverse activities (Marshall et al., 1999; Jenkins, 1990). The possibility of greater participation in more meaningful activities is often included in these invitations. Specific consequences for not participating in routines are not emphasized. Consequences for problem behavior that contribute to a sense of shame are specifically prohibited, as are predetermined consequences (e.g., "each use of profanity results in a day of no activities off-campus and 50 cents off your allowance"). It has been our experience that students perceive these pre-determined consequences to be little more than the staff's inability to understand the immediate problem and offer a solution (Garland & Dougher, 1991, referenced in Marshall et al., 1999). The staff then appears to be a provider of bad news and inflexibility. To the student who is amenable for treatment, this has the effect of punishing him for that which he has already acknowledged he needs to change (Marshall et al., 1999; Yager, Knight, Arnold, & Kempe, 1999).

Without the use of negative interventions and consequences, the staff's best tool is the use of engagement. All staff are trained that the development of healthy relationships is a fundamental element of their job. The daily life in the program consists of offering students the opportunity to be a productive member of whatever activities are available. It is stressed that the students should be given a range of options and invited to make the best decision they can. Under these circumstances, the student actively participates rather than being coerced into compliance.

Just as therapists are trained in therapeutic engagement, the staff are trained in styles conducive to nonthreatening invitation to participate in routines. This can take a wide range of forms, and includes specific training around the best possible use of praise and compliments to highlight the daily successes in students' lives (see Salter, 1995, pp. 182-183).

Sexual behavior problems are addressed specifically only in private settings. Residential treatment can be notorious for inadvertently publicizing private areas of children's lives. Within the intimate walls of a school or dormitory, it is easy for adults to forget the deeply personal nature of students' treatment goals. Harmful examples include open and public reference to a student's physical conditions such as bed-wetting or suspected victim-access behaviors. Further, knowledge of private matters can be used by students against each other. The staff at Bennington School are trained to recognize that discussions around personal affairs, including references towards sexual behavior problems, belong in a private area, preferably with the dorm supervisor, head teacher, or clinician.

This is done as much to educate students around healthy interpersonal boundaries as to reduce the secondary gain and arousal that can occur in such discussions.

Matter-of-fact stance. We have found this to be a key element in both therapeutic engagement and the management of daily routines (Yager et al., 1999). Maintaining a calm and matter-of-fact stance towards problematic behavior and situations reduces the extent of chaos and hysteria that students can experience and create. Examples of this include:

* Setting the same limit repeatedly in the same tone of voice to make clear that the staff will not become agitated or escalated;
* Addressing fundamental elements of a situation rather than the chaotic elements, e.g., "Hurting yourself is not allowed at Bennington School" or "I can't take you off-campus if you're assaultive towards others."

Treatment is driven by the needs of the student. Not all students who require residential treatment to address sexual behavior issues are able to immediately participate in a group therapy situation or even acknowledge their actions in an individual therapy setting (Yager et al., 1999; Salter, 1995). Many students are better able to address issues around their own victimization before they can address the damaging and hurtful behavior they have done to others.

Controversy has historically surrounded addressing victimization issues at the same time as perpetration issues. Many professionals (in personal communications) have viewed this as collusion, allowing the offender to make excuses, or dismissal of responsibility. We have found that working in individual therapy can prepare students for the work they will do in offense-specific group therapy. Once students have been provided this opportunity, they are often more willing and able to make a distinction between the issues and taking responsibility for their actions actually becomes easier. At the same time, the focus on personal responsibility espoused in group therapy enables them to address their victimization in individual therapy more effectively (Jenkins, 1990).

In other circumstances, students present in such deep shame around their behavior that placement in offense-specific treatment would be detrimental. In these situations every attempt is made throughout the day to engage them in activities which promote self-esteem and a sense of productivity and competence. The student who discovers he can be a hard worker in a prevocational setting discovers newer strength, courage, and an ethic that will enable his successful integration into treatment. In some instances, students who have been allowed these opportunities have become leaders in group therapy situations. In most cases the axiom has held true that *the slower you go the faster you get where you're going.*

Staff are trained to become aware of (and reduce) coercion. Understanding a continuum of coercion ranging from subtle bribery to force enables staff to invite rather than demand responsible behavior (Johnson, 1997; Jenkins, 1990). Mistakes are used as examples of how coercion and aggression can exist at small levels. The following examples may illustrate the point:

- *Favors and expectations of reciprocity.* A tired, frustrated line worker says, "I've been helping you guys out all day long, and this is what I get in return?" Students do not owe staff any favors. Rather, they owe it to themselves to manage their own lives and must be invited to do so in any number of creative ways.
- *Bribery.* "Do a good job with this and I'll take you out for lunch." This statement turns productivity from a source of pride to the pursuit of material gain. In the reverse, students who say, "take me out for lunch," are sometimes told, "How about if we just spend time together?"
- *Spontaneous punishment and revenge.* "If you can't behave in the cafeteria, then we'll leave you in the dorm with a staff and bring you back something to eat." This can reinforce the student's self-perception as incompetent and out of control. The staff should invite the student to behave and outline what is expected before going to the cafeteria. He should then manage whatever problems arise. Punishing the student teaches him little and does not facilitate substantive progress. Rather, should continued inability to succeed occur, a team decision to change the student's circumstances can be made in such a way that the youth may experience success.

These examples serve to illustrate how coercive treatment risks replication of abusive environments that the students were removed from (see Salter, 1995, pp. 175-83). Threats and bribery are among the hallmarks of abusive adults (Salter, 1995). Although students may understand and respond to coercion, it is ultimately shortsighted and neglects developmental needs (Ryan et al., 1999; Ryan & Lane, 1997).

Students are re-engaged rather than punished. It has been this author's experience that many adults can become confused in separating "consequences" from punishment. Adults often justify punishment as "holding" youth "accountable." Punishment is often used to alleviate anger at youth who are doing what they already acknowledge are treatment issues.

Statements such as "You haven't earned a home visit" and "You need to deal with this right now" create obligations that needn't exist. Usually, such approaches have not worked in other settings such as the child's home and school. It may be grandiose to believe that they will work in the present.

Another example of institutional punishment exists in formalized "consequences" applied uniformly despite the characteristics of the individual. A mandatory sentence of being restricted to campus for 3 days following a defiant act precludes re-engaging that student. Occasionally students in residential treatment are assigned consequences due to continue beyond their discharge date.

The following scenario illustrates a more positive approach. Several hours before a long-awaited softball game, A and B run away from the program for about one hour and are returned by the police. A is defiant and says that given the opportunity he will do it again. B expresses considerable regret and understands that he will be (quite naturally) under more intensive supervision for the foreseeable future. If a uniform sanction is applied to both students, the question arises as to who gains? This shortsighted approach misses a strong opportunity to reintegrate a student back into treatment. A will continue to be defiant, and B will continue to experience shame. A more effective approach to these students is to keep A under close supervision with a staff person until he can be trusted not to run away. He will always have the opportunity for reintegration when he is able to be direct and genuine with others. B will go off to the softball game where it is understood he will be watched closely.

The primary underlying ethic in this and other situations is that while safety and accountability are of primary importance, it is possible to administer "natural consequences" in a way that is benevolent and generous and demonstrates the same values to the child.

A concern is often raised that it is difficult to hold students accountable for their actions when so many of their actions appear (falsely) to be "forgiven" or ignored. It may be said that rather than "holding" students accountable through artificial means, the staff are teaching students how to develop accountability. This often takes longer to achieve than assigning accountability, but in our experience has taught students skills for responsible life.

Jargon is strongly discouraged. Residential treatment centers often develop their own language. Idioms and technical language replace clear, direct, genuine communication. Just as swearing is an aggressive act which eventually reduces one's ability to communicate effectively, staff are always at risk to fall back on familiar patterns of speech that ultimately lose substance and meaning. Students may respond by memorizing the words rather than their meaning. A focus on clinical language rarely inspires the student to develop a new sense of identity for himself. Instead, a premium is placed on communication that is expressed directly, assertively, genuinely, and respectfully.

Staff are trained in the artful use of praise. Praise is a sensitive topic to youth with sexual behavior problems and to abused youth in general. After all, children who have been sexually abused have most likely been praised either as a victim access technique or following the abuse (Salter, 1995). Often it is questioned whether an abused child can trust generic praise at all. Statements such as "nice job" have little meaning and can appear disingenuous or manipulative. Praise that describes in detail how a student's actions contribute to his own success or that of the community has more meaning. Praise may have more meaning still when it is clearly broadcast to others through a genuine awards ceremony or school newspaper.

Line staff are held to professional standards and honored. Line staff in residential treatment have highly challenging jobs. Across the profession burnout can be high and wages low. In treatment centers where equal value is not assigned to each department there can be a sense among staff that clinical interventions are somehow more important than direct intervention around daily routines and activities. This can occur despite the reality that attending to the simple tasks and obligations of daily life is therapeutic in its own right (Fuente & Wand, 1999).

Bennington School staff are reminded wherever possible that the work they do with students is professional, honorable, therapeutic, and important. They are offered access to continued education and conferences specific to their work. They are further invited to view themselves as professionals and are held to the same standards as any other department.

Students participate in planning for their treatment and discharge. If students are to take responsibility for their actions and lives, they must experience a meaningful role in the treatment process. Treatment plans are written in simple language to enable maximum participation from students.

Supervision is expressed as a part of safety. Intensive supervision of youth with sexual behavior problems is of obvious importance (particularly in preventing relapse). However, supervision can be administered in coercive and manipulative ways. Supervision at Bennington School is provided in such a way that projects prosocial values. The staff are trained to provide supervision by being with students at all times. Students who are within eyesight but out of earshot are not being supervised. Supervision that stresses engagement also eases the burden of peer pressure and reduces the exchange of antisocial attitudes among students (Fuente & Wand, 1999; Dishion, McCord, & Poulin, 1999).

CONCLUSIONS

There is a significant lack of literature regarding residential treatment programs for youth who have sexually abused (Curwen, 2000). In treating juveniles with sexual behavior problems we must be prepared to treat a wide variety of domains (Ryan et al., 1999). The actions of treatment providers must be tailored in such a way that invites responsibility (Jenkins, 1990), creates an orientation for the student toward his own future (Ryan et al., 1999), and helps him explore and establish a newer identity for himself. This can be accomplished more effectively by identifying and abandoning coercive and aggressive elements of treatment (Ryan & Lane, 1997; Ryan et al., 1999; Jenkins, 1990; Marshall, Anderson, & Fernandez, 1999). While seductive and effective for a short duration, coercion does not teach youth how to rebuild their lives. It is shortsighted and meets the needs of adults more than the children whose identities are under their care (Garland & Dougher, 1991, referenced in Marshall, Anderson, & Fernandez, 1999).

Treatment marked by invitation, engagement, relationships, and education can be extremely difficult to initiate. It requires skill, training, inexhaustible creativity, kindness, and optimism. It can be confusing to those who view their jobs as holding youth accountable rather than teaching accountability through kindness, words, and action.

However, the dividends for the students are quite high. They are able to explore and develop themselves rather than work their way through a system. They are better able to generate benevolence, having been the recipients of kindness. They are better able to give because they have been given to.

REFERENCES

Alexander, M. (1999). Sexual Offender Treatment Efficacy Revisited, *Sexual Abuse: A Journal of Research and Treatment, 11*, 110-116.

Barbaree, H., & Cortoni, F.A. (1993). Treatment of the Juvenile Sex Offender within the Criminal Justice and Mental Health Systems, in Barbaree, H., Marshall, W., & Hudson, S. (eds.), *The Juvenile Sex Offender*. New York: Guilford Press.

Barbaree, H., Marshall, W., & Hudson, S. (1993). *The Juvenile Sex Offender*. New York: Guilford Press.

Cavanagh, Johnson, T. , & Associates (1997). *Sexual, Physical and Emotional Abuse in Out-of-Home Care*. New York: The Haworth Press, Inc.

Dishion, T.J., McCord, J., & Poulin, F. (1999). When Interventions Harm: Peer Groups and Problem Behavior. *American Psychologist, 54*, 755-764.

Elliott, D.S. (1994). The Developmental Course of Sexual and Non-Sexual Violence: Results from a National Longitudinal Study. Paper presented at the meeting of the Association for the Treatment of Sexual Abusers' 13th Annual Research and Treatment Conference, San Francisco.

Forth, A.E., & Burke, H.C. (1998). Psychopathy in Adolescence: Assessment, Violence, and Developmental Precursors, in Cooke, D.J., Forth, A.E., & Hare, R.D., *Psychopathy: Theory, Research, and Implications for Society*. Dordrecht, The Netherlands: Kluwer.

Fuente, T., & Wand, S. (1999). Therapeutic Intervention as Mediation of Subsequent Life Experience, in Ryan, G. & Associates (eds.), *Web of Meaning: A Developmental-Contextual Approach in Sexual Abuse Treatment*. Brandon, VT: Safer Society Press.

Frick, P. (1998). *Conduct Disorder and Severe Antisocial Behavior*. New York: Plenum Press.

Hubble, M.A., Duncan, B.L., & Miller, S.C. (1999). *The Heart and Soul of Change: What Works in Therapy*. Washington, DC: American Psychological Association.

Hunter, J. (1999). Understanding Juvenile Sexual Offending Behavior: Emerging Research, Treatment Approaches, and Management Practices. Center for Sex Offender Management, and available at http://www.csom.org

Jenkins, Alan (1990). *Invitations to Responsibility*. Adelaide, Australia: Dulwich Centre Publications.

Loeber, R., & Farrington, D.P. (1998). *Serious and Violent Juvenile Offenders*. London: Sage Publishing.

Marshall, W.L., Anderson, D., & Fernandez, Y. (1999). *Cognitive Behavioural Treatment of Sexual Offenders*. Chichester, UK: Wiley.

Perry, G. & Orchard, L. (1992). *Assessment and Treatment of Adolescent Sex Offenders*. Sarasota, FL: Professional Resource Press.

Prentky, R., Harris, B., Frizzell, K., & Righthand, S. (2000). An Actuarial Procedure for Assessing Risk with Juvenile Sex Offenders. *Sexual Abuse: A Journal of Research and Treatment, 12*, 71-93.

Prentky, R. (2000). Juvenile Sex Offender Assessment Protocol (JSOAP). Presentation at Sinclair Seminars' Sex Offender Re-Offense Risk Prediction Symposium, Madison, WI, March, 2000.

Ryan, G., & Lane, S. (1997). *Juvenile Sexual Offending: Causes, Consequences, and Correction*. San Francisco: Jossey-Bass.

Ryan, G. & Associates (1999). *Web of Meaning: A Developmental-Contextual Approach in Sexual Abuse Treatment*. Brandon, VT: Safer Society Press.

Salter, A.C. (1988). *Treating Child Sex Offenders and Victims*. Newbury Park, CA: Sage Publications.

Salter, A.C. (1995). *Transforming Trauma*. Thousand Oaks, CA: Sage Publications.

Weinrott, M.R. (1996). *Juvenile Sexual Aggression: A Critical Review*. Boulder, CO: Center for the Study and Prevention of Violence.

Worling, J.R. Beyond the Looking Glass: Predicting Adolescent Sex Offender Recidivism from the Results of a 10-Year Treatment Study. Paper presented at the 18th Annual Research and Treatment Conference, Association for the Treatment of Sexual Abusers, Lake Buena Vista, FL, September 1999.

Yager, J., Knight, L., Arnold, L., & Kempe, R. (1999). The Discovery Process, in Ryan, G. & Associates (eds.), *Web of Meaning: A Developmental-Contextual Approach in Sexual Abuse Treatment*. Brandon, VT: Safer Society Press.

Circles of Support:
A Restorative Justice Initiative

Robin J. Wilson, PhD, CPsych
Michelle Prinzo, MA

SUMMARY. This paper addresses the increasing difficulties faced in community-based management of sexual offenders in Canada. Those offenders at particularly high-risk to re-offend (e.g., sadistic rapists and serial child molesters) often receive indeterminate sentences, and are rarely released to the community prior to death or incapacitating illness. However, many other high-risk offenders are released from custody at the end of a determinate sentence, often without the benefit of adequate supervision or treatment. In a restorative justice initiative managed by the Mennonite Central Committee of Ontario, 30 high-risk sexual offenders released at sentence completion were provided with community support in the form of Circles of Support and Accountability. A brief overview of the Canadian penal system and its handling of sexual offenders is given to provide the social and political framework in which many current restorative justice projects have been undertaken. It is ar-

Robin J. Wilson is affiliated with the Correctional Service of Canada, Central Ontario District (Parole), 330 Keele Street, Main Floor, Toronto, Ontario, M6P 2K7 Canada. Michelle Prinzo is affiliated with the Ontario Correctional Institute, Brampton, Ontario, Canada.

The authors would like to thank Andrew J. R. Harris for his comments on an earlier version of the manuscript.

The views expressed herein do not necessarily represent those of the Correctional Service of Canada, the Ministry of the Solicitor General and Correctional Services, or the Governments of Ontario and Canada.

[Haworth co-indexing entry note]: "Circles of Support: A Restorative Justice Initiative." Wilson, Robin J., and Michelle Prinzo. Co-published simultaneously in *Journal of Psychology & Human Sexuality* (The Haworth Press, Inc.) Vol. 13, No. 3/4, 2001, pp. 59-77; and: *Sex Offender Treatment: Accomplishments, Challenges, and Future Directions* (ed: Michael H. Miner, and Eli Coleman) The Haworth Press, Inc., 2001, pp. 59-77. Single or multiple copies of this article are available for a fee from The Haworth Document Delivery Service [1-800-HAWORTH, 9:00 a.m. - 5:00 p.m. (EST). E-mail address: getinfo@haworthpressinc.com].

59

gued that traditional punitive measures have done little to address risk to the community and that effective interventions in the community must not be limited to time under warrant. The Circles of Support initiative focuses on the need to engage the community in the offender reintegration process. Data are provided regarding recidivism rates in comparison to actuarial projections determined from STATIC-99 (Hanson & Thornton, 1999) survival curves. Recidivism across 30 high-risk offenders, with a mean follow-up time of 36 months, currently stands at less than 40% of that predicted by STATIC-99. *[Article copies available for a fee from The Haworth Document Delivery Service: 1-800-HAWORTH. E-mail address: <getinfo@haworthpressinc.com> Website: <http://www.HaworthPress.com> © 2001 by The Haworth Press, Inc. All rights reserved.]*

KEYWORDS. Sexual offenders, restorative justice, community management, supervision

INTRODUCTION

The punishment and rehabilitation of offenders has been the subject of much recent debate in popular and scholarly circles in many nations of the world, particularly as the discussion pertains to sex offenders. International symposia, such as the 6th International Conference on the Treatment of Sex Offenders (during which the following paper was presented), have been convened to stimulate dialogue regarding the safe and ethical risk management of sexual offenders. While the goal of all parties concerned is the prevention of further victimization, the means by which individual nations or jurisdictions strive to achieve that goal have been varied.

Although much of the discussion regarding offender risk management has focused on traditional methods of correctional sanction, rehabilitative programming, and psychological or psychiatric treatment, there has been a recent trend towards investigation of alternative methods of furthering reintegration of offenders released to the community. Collectively, a group of these alternative methods have come under the heading "restorative justice," although some might challenge the actual linkages between various initiatives. Overall, the restorative justice movement is one that seeks to facilitate the restoration of offenders to communities by combining education, support, and accountability, for both offenders and members of the community-at-large. The following paper discusses a Canadian restorative justice initiative intended to facilitate community reintegration of high-risk sexual offenders. However, we would like to start with a brief history of the management of offenders in Canada, as a means to set the stage for our presentation of the initiative proper.

Early attempts to maintain law and order in Canada may be seen as being directly descendent from practices originating in England and France, the two nations which primarily colonized what later became Canada. Prior to the 18th Century, the response to criminal offenders in Canada focused largely on corporal punishment. During the 18th Century, there was a transition from corporal punishment to imprisonment as the sanction of choice. Imprisonment in workhouses was established as the primary mode of punishment in many provinces. In these workhouses, prisoners were employed to perform labour jobs within the institution. Persons awaiting trial or those awaiting sentencing were held in gaols.

Over the period of 1790-1830, major shifts occurred in the perception of crime and the roots of criminal behavior. Crime came to be viewed as a consequence of community disorder and family instability (Griffiths & Cunningham, 2000). The Canadian Penitentiary Act of 1834 emphasized the use of penitentiaries as a general deterrent and as a mechanism for reforming criminals through hard labour. Reflecting the origin of the word "penitentiary," religion was a focal point and moral reeducation of inmates was strongly encouraged. Hard labour was also used.

In 1835, Kingston Penitentiary (Canada's first) opened its doors in Ontario. But by 1840, concerns arose regarding the effectiveness of punishing and reforming offenders. Recidivism rates were high and there was extensive use of corporal punishment inside the facility. The Penitentiary Act of 1851 reflected calls for improvement in institutional conditions and to deal with offender needs in more effective and humane ways.

During the 1870s, various prisons were constructed across Canada. The 1889 Act to Permit the Conditional Release of First Offenders in Certain Cases introduced the practice of releasing offenders on their own recognizance rather than imposing a sentence. Probation was first mentioned in revisions to the Criminal Code of Canada in 1892. Changes to the Code in 1921 required offenders to report to an officer of the court. This "probation" became the cornerstone of what has become "community corrections" in Canada.

In Canada, jurisdiction regarding supervision of offenders is split between the provinces and the federal government. Unlike the United

States, where jurisdiction is determined by offense type, Canadian offenders are routed to provincial or federal supervision based solely on the length of sentence to be served. Sentences of less than two years (i.e., two years less a day, or under) are administered by the province in which the offense occurred, while offenders serving sentences of two years or more fall under federal jurisdiction. All probationary sentences are supervised by the provincial correctional service.

Currently, the majority of Canada's federal offender population achieves conditional release at some point during their sentence, be that Day Parole, Full Parole, or Statutory Release. Parole is roughly equivalent to earned remission or "time off for good behavior," and is granted by the National Parole Board, which is independent from the correctional service. Statutory Release (SR) is mandated in law, but may be suspended (i.e., this keeps the offender in prison) for those who meet rigorous criteria demonstrating that some undue risk is posed to community safety. Those offenders who achieve conditional release are supervised by a parole officer who ensures adherence to release conditions imposed by the National Parole Board.

Although conditional release in Canada has a long history, recent shifts in policy reflect the community's increasing intolerance for criminal behavior, particularly in regard to sexual offenders. The sociopolitical pendulum has swung back to punishment, away from rehabilitation. Public outcry has led to political responses such as longer sentences, more stringent criteria for granting conditional release, and measures to enhance supervision in the community. Accordingly, there has been a decline over the past decade in the proportion of federal offenders afforded community supervision (Correctional Service of Canada, 2000). As a result, fewer federal offenders achieve conditional release prior to their Statutory Release Date, and many SR candidates are being detained until sentence completion (or Warrant Expiry Date–WED). This is particularly true for sexual offenders.

Although maintaining offenders in prison for longer periods of time may satisfy some of the public's belief that offenders require punishment and a significant period of removal from society, the practice of limiting community supervision is a proverbial double-edged sword. Indeed, research shows that the availability of facilitated community reintegration significantly impacts risk for future involvement in criminal activities, with those offenders receiving community support being at less risk for recidivism (Andrews & Bonta, 1998; Wilson, Stewart, Stirpe, Barrett, & Cripps, 2000). Andrews and Bonta (1998) have clearly shown that imprisonment without appropriate rehabilitative services amounts to a virtual "deep freeze," in which offenders are returned to the community slightly worse than when they went in. Conversely, interventions which attend to risk levels, criminogenic needs, and offender responsivity can significantly increase success on release. Traditionally, offenders released at WED have not had the benefit of services (e.g., treatment, advocacy) available to conditionally released offenders. This is in clear contradiction to the research noted above.

Sexual Offenders

The Criminal Code of Canada has undergone numerous modifications during the 20th century. However, it was not until the 1970s that changes were made regarding the classification of sexual offenses as crimes of violence. These changes reflected the public's call for clearer definitions of offenses, appropriate sentencing, and rules governing evidence and legal proceedings. For example, prior to 1976, Common Law rules allowed evidence pertaining to the woman's sexual and moral character to be entered as evidence for the defense. As such, the trial process was often biased against the victim, in that it was assumed that the victim had likely consented to the particular act in question if she had previously consented to sexual activity with the accused. In 1976, amendments were made to the Criminal Code of Canada providing that no questions could be asked about the sexual conduct of the complainant with other people unless "reasonable notice" had been given to the courts. This has been colloquially referred to as the "rape shield."

In 1978, the Law Reform Commission of Canada (LRCC–see review in Holden, 1999, available from the present authors) published a working paper which gathered the majority of sexual offenses (e.g., rape, indecent exposure, indecent assault) together under the general crime of "sexual assault." Sexual Assault, as defined by the LRCC, would be committed if a person had sexual contact with another person without consent. The recommendations of the LRCC were enacted in 1983, and comprised the first major attempt to operationalize the Canadian legal community's definition and handling of sexual offenses and offenders. Since that time, other legislation has been enacted to further clarify the Criminal Code of Canada sections related to sexual offenses. Subsequent laws have dealt with protection of victim rights, the reporting and prosecution of sexual assaults, victim impact statements, and definitions of consent.

Presently, penalties for sexual offenses range from six months to life imprisonment. Substantial changes in regard to correctional policies were reflected in the Corrections and Conditional Release Act (CCRA) of 1992. The CCRA set out policy and guidelines for correctional services and parole boards in their dealings with offenders. One specific change was in regard to detention provisions, in that the Act made it easier to detain sex offenders, particularly those who committed crimes against children. One of the two criteria for detention states that if "the offense was a sexual offense involving a child and there are reasonable grounds to believe that the offender is likely to commit a sexual offense involving a child before expiration of the offender's sentence according to law" then a referral for detention will be considered.

Many jurisdictions in Canada (and, indeed, other countries) have experienced the difficulties associated with high profile cases of sexual assault or sex offender recidivism. It would appear that the public's sentiments towards sexual offenders are hardening and, as such, policy changes have resulted in more restrictive measures for many sexual offenders. In particular, more Canadian sexual offenders are being declared "dangerous offenders" (DOs), a legal definition which provides for the imposition of an indeterminate sentence for repeat, serious offenders and, in particular, sexual offenders. Experience has shown that few DOs are ever granted conditional release and, thus, serve 100% of their sentences in penitentiaries. For those serious offenders not meeting the DO standard, the courts now have the additional option of imposing Long Term Offender (LTO) designations, which consist of up to 10 years of post-sentence community supervision. Of those offenders not designated as DOs or LTOs, many more are being detained to WED in accordance with provisions of the CCRA.

While the result of the policy changes noted above has been that sexual offenders are removed from society for longer periods, there are considerable concerns regarding the larger implications of such legislation. In particular, resources in the community (e.g., parole supervision, counselling, psychoeducational programming) are normally linked to a supervising agency, like the Correctional Service of Canada (CSC). Offenders released at WED have not traditionally had the benefit of access to community reintegration services. Over the years, community-based management of sexual offenders has become an increasingly public affair, to the extent that many jurisdictions now have policies regarding public notification, sex offender registration, and provision of DNA samples. In Canada, sex offenders comprise 24% of all federal inmates. National Parole Board statistics reveal that the percentage of prisoners in the total prison population actually referred for detention increased from 4.3% in 1989-1990 to 10.2% in 1994-1995 (Mennonite Central

Committee, 1996). The majority of the difference is attributable to increased detention rates for sexual offenders.

Policy documents of the Correctional Service of Canada define community reintegration as "all activity and programming conducted to prepare an offender to return safely to the community and live as a law-abiding citizen" (Thurber, 1998). CSC personnel use offender-specific information, including static and dynamic risk determinants, in their efforts to reduce risk for re-offense. Comprehensive data management allows for actuarial assessment, and also serves to better inform parole supervisors about offender functioning in the community. Such data are crucial for program development and implementation, as well as the formulation of correctional plans for individual offenders. These measures help offenders to reintegrate to society while allowing for enhanced monitoring of offense-specific behavior patterns. Close supervision of precursors to offending allows for therapeutic suspension of conditional release, and periodic revocation where indicated. If an offender is detained until WED, the community loses the ability to monitor these variables and, subsequently, the spirit of reintegration is defeated.

In the past, decision makers were forced to rely on clinical judgments rendered by professionals; however, the average predictive accuracy of such judgments in predicting sex offence recidivism has been shown to be only slightly better than chance (Hanson & Thornton, 1999). Increasingly, the decision to detain an offender is determined using empirically-derived, standardized procedures and resultant actuarial measures (Hanson, 2000). However, despite advances in this domain (e.g., STATIC-99–Hanson & Thornton, 1999), the procedures used in determining risk are still subject to limitations of reliability and validity. Notwithstanding recent findings and innovations in sex offender risk assessment, much debate remains in the literature regarding how risk should be assessed and managed.

Hanson and Bussière (1998) conducted a rigorous meta-analysis of the predictors of sexual recidivism, the results of which suggest that sex offence recidivism is closely related to sexual deviance. The strongest predictors were positive phallometric assessments, a history of sex offences, and a history of diverse sexual crimes. They also found that sexual recidivism was associated with prior nonsexual offences and a diagnosis of Antisocial Personality Disorder (particularly, those extreme cases of APD commonly thought to be reflective of psychopathy–Hare, 1993). The meta-analysis also revealed that predictors of general and non-sexual violent recidivism were similar to predictors of general recidivism among non-sexual criminals. Almost all predictors of sexual offence recidivism were historical or stable (i.e., unlikely to change, regardless of the intervention employed). The most changeable risk factor was motivation for treatment, in that offenders who rejected or performed poorly in treatment were at higher risk to re-offend.

The Rise of Restorative Justice

Over the last 10 years, "restorative justice" has been widely recognized in Canadian public discourse (Roach, 2000). This has happened as many nations grapple with burgeoning prison populations and the difficulties associated with returning previously incarcerated persons to increasingly intolerant communities. Those at the forefront of the restorative justice vanguard assert that any successful reintegration of offenders to the community must include active participation of all community stakeholders. This has been, at times, a bitter pill for fearful citizens to swallow, particularly in regard to sexual offenders.

Although restorative justice is not a new concept in Canada, it was never fully embraced until sentencing reforms were made in 1996. Earlier committees had acknowledged the potential for use of such principles, but the 1996 reforms were the first to recognize the restorative concept that the provision of reparations to victims and the community are legitimate goals of sentencing (*Martin's Annual Criminal Code*, 1999). Since those reforms, restorative justice continued to rise in criminal justice discourse, and can be seen in decisions made by the Supreme Court of Canada (see review in Roach, 2000).

The multiple purposes of sentencing, which include rehabilitation, deterrence, incapacitation, and retribution, have resulted in a great deal of subjectivity in regard to sentencing decisions by judges. Adding restorative justice opportunities to the mix is likely to exacerbate this difficulty but, nonetheless, represents a potential for transforming the way in which we deal with offenders and the goals of sentencing. The concept of restorative justice includes important principles such as fairness, equality, accountability, reparation, forgiveness, inclusion, and healing. In traditional criminal justice systems, justice is used to heal victims and requires that all stakeholders have an opportunity to be involved in harm assessment and reduction (Miller & Schacter, 2000).

The Law Commission of Canada outlines three fundamental principles of restorative justice:

1. crime is a violation of a relationship among victims, offenders, and the community;
2. restoration involves the victim, the offender, and community members; and
3. a consensus approach should be used in the application of justice. (Roach, 2000)

The Supreme Court of Canada has ruled that restorative sanctions can achieve the multiple purposes of punishment, including denunciation, deterrence, proportionality, and rehabilitation (*R. v. Gladue*; see Roach, 2000).

Restorative justice is often defined and used as a means to promote accountability of offenders for crime. Offenders are encouraged to accept responsibility and to face the victims of their crime, as well as other members of the community. Some argue that accountability is a more meaningful response in acknowledging the consequences of crime than are short terms of imprisonment. Accepting responsibility and making amends are key features of restorative justice. These are also particularly helpful in establishing workable offender reintegration programs.

Restorative justice has also shown that rehabilitation of offenders is an important and achievable goal. The 1970s saw a decline in the support for rehabilitation of offenders, as many subscribed to the "nothing works" philosophy (Martinson, 1974; Roach, 2000). Many continue to adhere to this doctrine, in spite of evidence to the contrary (Gendreau, Smith, & Goggin, in press; Hanson, 2000). Further, the Supreme Court of Canada has defended the efforts of restorative justice and identified that rehabilitation does not end in prison, but that community participation in justice, including treatment, and the participation of families and the community at large, plays a pivotal role.

To summarize, restorative justice is defended as a more effective means of crime prevention than punitive approaches (Roach, 2000). The focus is on the specific deterrence of offenders such that an offender who is restored, or is on the road to restoration, is less likely to re-offend. Further, restorative justice initiatives act as a general deterrent in that they serve to increase community involvement regarding, and monitoring of, particular behaviors in particular communities. Restorative justice in Canada is continuing to grow in its appeal, as community groups, victims, women, and Aboriginal peoples continue to work together to help restorative principles gain acceptance by criminal justice professionals.

Circles of Support and Accountability

Notwithstanding the advances reported above, risk assessment continues to be an inexact science and complete accuracy is likely unobtainable. With that in mind, it is unlikely that the public will tolerate even the comparatively small recidivism rates to which innovations in risk assessment and community supervision and treatment strategies have contributed (Wilson, Kirkegaard, & Heise, 1998). In essence, without the ability to completely eradicate recidivism, communities will continue to call for measures to keep high-risk offenders away. Nonetheless, most sexual offenders are serving determinate sentences, and will face reentry to the community at some point. As noted above, those offenders detained to WED are released with few structured supports to assist in their reintegration, with the end result being that there are no additional safeguards for the public other than those afforded by the police. Such offenders are not bound by any release conditions, are not supervised by parole or probation officers and, at present, are not routinely required to inform law enforcement of their residence or activities. Efforts to address the latter point, using Megan's Law in the United States as a model, are presently before the Ontario Legislature. Presently, police may apply to the court to have peace bonds imposed on certain offenders, which allows for the imposition of conditions for remaining in the community.

The Community Reintegration Project (CRP–Mennonite Central Committee, 1996) was specifically conceived to address the needs of communities by providing outreach to high-risk sex offenders released at WED and by providing a framework for the formation of Circles of Support and Accountability. The purpose of the CRP is to speak to the fears of victims, to reduce the risk of re-offence, and to ease offenders' transition from institutional to community settings. Circles of Support are intended to provide the development of a relapse prevention team for an ex-offender. A typical circle is comprised of concerned citizens (volunteers) who have a common interest in helping to prevent further sexual victimization through guidance, advocacy and monitoring of offender activities in the community. The circle has the dual responsibility of providing a caring community for the core member (i.e., the offender) while striving to increase community safety. A graphic representation of a Circle of Support is shown in Figure 1.

The primary initiative of the CRP is a pilot project set up for South-Central Ontario involving recruitment of volunteers from the community to form Circles of Support around high-risk/high-profile

FIGURE 1. Relationships of the Circle Within the Community

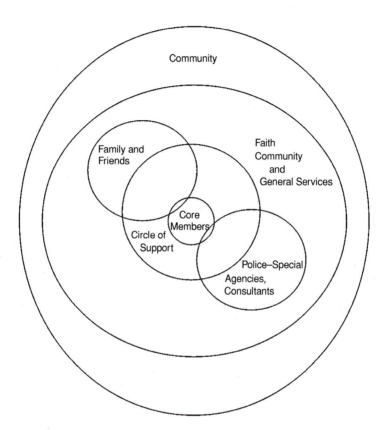

sex offenders. Circles provide intensive support for the core member to assist in a safe, orderly adjustment to everyday life in the community. In order to achieve this, Circle members must fulfil many roles:

1. Circle members function as advocates, working to increase cooperation with police, victims, treatment providers, and the community.
2. They confront the core member about those attitudes and behaviors which put him at risk for relapse.
3. Members are available to assist the core member through emergencies.

4. As part of the greater community, Circle members mediate community concerns.
5. Circle members encourage and join the core member in celebrating anniversaries, milestones, and other victories in their reintegration.

Optimal circle size is four to six community volunteers, in order to provide a variety of opinions. Members of circles have included members of faith congregations, police officers, psychologists, family medical practitioners, and community advocates. All Circle volunteers are screened and informed of the initial one-year commitment. The first two months of any Circle are usually intense, involving one to two contacts with the core member per week. Depending on the offender and his needs, daily contact may be required during the period immediately following release. The full Circle meets weekly and once the core member adjusts to his new life in the community, meetings are reduced to twice monthly. To be effective in the reintegration process, Circles should meet on an as-needed basis. It is expected that some Circles will be maintained for several years, reflecting the reality that, for some offenders, reintegration is a long-term process. To date, 30 Circles have been undertaken in South-Central Ontario, as part of the pilot project. Circles have been undertaken in other parts of Canada; however, data regarding their success or failure will not be presented here.

METHOD

Subjects

Subjects were 30 federally-sentenced, male sexual offenders detained until their warrant expiry date (demographic data are presented in Table 1). All subjects were identified by institutional staff as being at substantial risk to re-offend following release, hence the detention order by the National Parole Board. Each subject is currently, or has recently been, involved in a Circle of Support in South-Central Ontario, under the management of the Mennonite Central Committee of Ontario. Average time of follow-up, which is an approximation of the length of time of involvement in a Circle, is 36 months with the range being from 16 to 79 months.

TABLE 1. Group Demographics (N = 30)

M(SD) age in years	41.6 (11.65)
% deviant phallometrics	46.7
M(SD) STATIC-99	6.03 (2.17)
M(SD) RRASOR	3.17 (1.60)
M(SD) SORAG	17.30 (10.64)
Victims	
M number	2.8
% female only	53.3
% familial only	7.0
% children only	46.7
% Predicted survival (STATIC-99)	73.98
% Actual survival	90.0
M(SD) follow-up (months)	36 (14.84)
Range (months)	16 - 79

Actuarial Measures

The STATIC-99 (Hanson & Thornton, 1999) was created by adding together items from two previously-existing measures, the Rapid Risk Assessment of Sex Offender Recidivism (RRASOR–Hanson, 1997) and the Structured Anchored Clinical Judgement (SACJ–Grubin, 1998). The resultant scale was found to be more accurate in its predictive ability than either measure alone. Hanson and Thornton also showed that the STATIC-99 is more accurate than unstructured clinical judgment, and that it possesses moderate accuracy in predicting any violent recidivism among sex offenders.

The Sex Offender Risk Assessment Guide (SORAG–Quinsey, Harris, Rice, & Cormier, 1998) is an actuarial risk assessment tool devised by its authors to measure risk for recidivism by sexual offenders. It is similar in construction to the Violence Risk Appraisal Guide (VRAG–Quinsey et al., 1998). While the SORAG has no published validation data, the VRAG has demonstrated reasonable predictive validity with respect to potential for violent recidivism, including sexual re-offending.

The STATIC-99, RRASOR and the SORAG were completed for each offender after review of the documents and reports on the Offender Management System (OMS), the national offender data bank of the

Correctional Service of Canada. Each offender's level of risk was assessed by his scores on the STATIC-99, RRASOR, and SORAG (see Table 1). Once each offender's level of risk was calculated using the actuarial measures, survival analysis was used to estimate recidivism probabilities. Survival analysis calculates the probability of recidivating for each time period as long as the offender has not yet recidivated (Hanson & Thornton, 2000). Survival analysis was used due to its advantage of being able to estimate month-by-month recidivism projections when follow-up periods vary across offenders. Instances of recidivism were defined as charges or convictions recorded on an offender's criminal record.

RESULTS

Mean time at risk was 36 months with the range being from 16 months to just over six-and-a-half years. Average scores on the STATIC-99, RRASOR, and SORAG (N = 23) were 6.03, 3.12, and 17.30, respectively. These ratings confirm the higher risk status of offenders involved in the study. Using mean time at risk and average STATIC-99 score, in combination with established survival data (Hanson, personal communication), we predicted that approximately seven instances of sexual recidivism should have occurred in this group to date. Average expected survival over the 30 cases was 73.98% using the formula:

$$\Sigma \text{ (survival probabilities)}/N$$

However, only three persons have recidivated to date: one for indecent telephone calls, another for offenses against a child, and the last for sexual assault against a female adult. In each case, the offense committed was categorically less severe or invasive than the crime for which the offender had previously served a prison sentence. The difference between the expected survival and the observed survival in our sample was 16.02%. Using a z test with a correction for small sample (Hardyck & Petrinovich, 1969, pp. 167-169) in which the deviation of the observed survival proportion is compared to the expected survival proportion, based on Hanson's data, we were able to demonstrate a strong trend toward significance ($z = 1.79$, N = 30, $p < .075$).

DISCUSSION

This paper discusses a Canadian approach to restorative justice with conditionally-released, high-risk sexual offenders. Since the pilot program began, many others have "sprung up" around the nation. Further, members of our group have been invited to present the model in numerous international settings, including the United States, United Kingdom, and South Africa. Generally, the response has been favorable, indicating significant interest in the prospect of adding another dimension to the safe and ethical management of offenders.

The Circles of Support initiative uses community volunteers to aid in the management of sex offender risk. While these volunteers are screened and provided with training and support from professionals (e.g., psychologists, psychiatrists, etc.), and many of the volunteers are retired social service workers, the point is well taken that these are average community persons involved in a potentially dangerous enterprise. We argue, however, that the risk management provided by government agencies has fallen short of the needs of the community. This is particularly true of offenders released at sentence completion, usually to no treatment and no correctional supervision. Of those services that might be available through other agencies, decreases in funding and the resultant longer waiting lists have jeopardized community safety. Therefore, it is our position that the community must take a greater stake in ensuring its own safety. By including community members in the risk management process, we increase the level of understanding of the issues at hand, and empower citizens to be informed as to the risks present in their surroundings. While some may argue that this is fatalistic, we believe that an informed community is a safer community.

This study recorded scores on three actuarial sexual offense risk assessment measures (RRASOR, SORAG and STATIC-99), using the latter to predict estimated sexual recidivism rates. All three measures assessed the subjects to be high risk to re-offend sexually, demonstrating concurrent validity of the measures. This confirms earlier research in which the STATIC-99 predicted sex offense recidivism with similar levels of accuracy to the SORAG (Hanson & Thornton, 2000).

The results of comparisons between projected and actual recidivism show that the group of offenders included in this analysis are recidivating at a rate less than 40% of that expected using the STATIC-99 survival data provided by Hanson (personal communication). Of the 30 core members included in this study, only three have recidivated to date, while the probability was that seven would have done so. While it is possible that more offenders might have recidivated, the likelihood of that having occurred is decreased by the level of involvement of the Circle in the core member's life.

While difficult to determine conclusively, the strong trend toward significance in comparing the observed and expected recidivism proportions suggests that involvement in a Circle of Support has aided the offenders reported here in making a smoother transition to the community. Specifically, being held accountable for their actions, and being afforded a close community support network, has given them the kind of support that might have been available had they received conditional release. Results of a recently-reported investigation looking at recidivism rates for conditionally-released offenders to the same geographic area (Wilson et al., 2000) also suggested that collaborative facilitation of offender reintegration, including a variety of stakeholders, increases the likelihood of success. In that study, recidivism rates were also lower than those reported elsewhere in the literature (Barbaree, Seto, & Maric, 1996; Motiuk & Brown, 1996).

At present, the recidivism rates of our subject group have not been compared specifically to an analogous group released without the benefit of a Circle of Support. National data reported by Motiuk, Belcourt, and Bonta (1995) suggest that the sexual recidivism rate of detained sexual offenders is in line with, if not slightly higher than, the predictions made by the STATIC-99 survival data used here. It would be of interest to many to establish whether or not a statistically significant difference exists in regard to recidivism rates. However, Barbaree (1997) has suggested that, due to low base-rates, the demonstration of "treatment" effects is difficult. Nonetheless, this should not be seen as a rationale for discontinuing initiatives such as that detailed here. Indeed, Gendreau and his colleagues (in press) have ably demonstrated that small differences in recidivism rates have large social implications with respect to victim harm and a variety of cost indicators (e.g., trying, incarcerating, and treating offenders; and providing services for victims). The Circles of Support model might be of particular interest to those jurisdictions where the costs associated with maintaining offenders have grown unwieldy.

The current study used actuarial assessment, primarily of static variables, to predict a recidivism rate which was then compared to an actual recidivism rate. The reader is cautioned that, although certainly better than clinical judgment alone, actuarial assessment is also less than perfect. Hanson and Thornton acknowledge that the STATIC-99 provides only moderate predictive ability in regard to sexual or violent recidivism. Recent research (Hanson & Harris, 2000) has suggested that general risk assessment efforts would be greatly enhanced by consideration of dynamic factors, such as intimacy deficits, treatment failure, and non-cooperation with supervision. Hanson and Harris (2000) have recently introduced the Sex Offender Needs Assessment Rating, or SONAR, which attempts to accomplish the same goal as the STATIC-99, however, in regard to dynamic factors. While static indicators of risk have been traditionally viewed as superior in determining risk for re-offense, meta-analyses conducted by Gendreau, Little, and Goggin (1996) demonstrated that offender needs (or dynamic variables) are able to predict recidivism with similar strength. Dynamic factors are often more useful to treatment and supervisory personnel in managing offender risk in the community. We argue that Circles of Support are a good first step in including the community-at-large in risk management, and that they are a viable means to increase public safety.

REFERENCES

Andrews, D.A. & Bonta, J. (1998). *The psychology of criminal conduct, Second Edition.* Cincinnati, OH: Anderson.

Barbaree, H.E. (1997). Evaluating treatment efficacy with sexual offenders: The insensitivity of recidivism studies to treatment effectiveness. *Sexual Abuse, 9,* 111-128.

Barbaree, H.E., Seto, M.C., & Maric, A. (1996). Sex offender characteristics, response to treatment and correctional release decisions at the Warkworth Sexual Behaviour Clinic (*Working Papers in Impulsivity Research Report*). Toronto, ON: Clarke Institute of Psychiatry.

Correctional Service of Canada (2000). *The safe return of offenders to the community: Statistical Overview 2000.* Ottawa, ON: Research Branch, CSC. (available at www.csc-scc.gc.ca)

Gendreau, P., Little, T., & Goggin, C. (1996). A meta-analysis of the predictors of adult offender recidivism: What works? *Criminology, 34,* 575-607.

Gendreau, P., Smith, P., & Goggin, C. (in press). Treatment programs in corrections. In: J. Winterdyk (Ed.), *Corrections in Canada: Social reaction to crime.* Scarborough, ON: Prentice-Hall.

Griffiths, C. & Cunningham, A. (2000). *Canadian corrections.* Scarborough, ON: Nelson Thomas Learning.

Grubin, D. (1998). Sex offending against children: Understanding the risk (*Police Research Series Paper 99*). London: Home Office.

Hanson, R.K. (1997). The development of a brief actuarial risk scale for sexual offense recidivism (*User Report 1997-04*). Ottawa: ON: Department of the Solicitor General of Canada. (available at www.sgc.gc.ca)

Hanson, R.K. (2000). *Risk assessment: Prepared for the Association for the Treatment of Sex Abusers.* Beaverton, OR: ATSA.

Hanson, R.K. (2000, November). *The effectiveness of treatment for sexual offenders: Report of the ATSA Collaborative Research Committee.* Plenary address made at the 19th Annual Research and Treatment Conference of the Association for the Treatment of Sexual Abusers, San Diego, CA.

Hanson, R.K. & Bussière, M.T. (1996). Predictors of sexual offender recidivism: A meta-analysis (*User Report 1996-04*). Ottawa, ON: Department of the Solicitor General of Canada. (available at www.sgc.gc.ca)

Hanson, R.K. & Bussière, M.T. (1998). Predicting relapse: A meta-analysis of sexual offender recidivism studies. *Journal of Consulting and Clinical Psychology, 66,* 348-362.

Hanson, R.K. & Harris, A.J.R. (2000). *The Sex Offender Need Assessment Rating (SONAR): A method for measuring change in risk levels* (User Report 2000-1). Ottawa, ON: Department of the Solicitor General of Canada. (available at www. sgc.gc.ca)

Hanson, R.K. & Thornton, D. (1999). *Static-99: Improving actuarial risk assessments for sex offenders* (User Report 1999-02). Ottawa, ON: Department of the Solicitor General of Canada. (available at www.sgc.gc.ca)

Hanson, R.K. & Thornton, D. (2000). Improving risk assessments for sex offenders: A comparison of three actuarial scales. *Law and Human Behavior, 24,* 119-136.

Hardyck, C.D. & Petrinovich, L.F. (1969). *Introduction to statistics for the behavioral sciences.* Philadelphia, PA: W.B. Saunders.

Hare, R. (1993). *Without conscience.* New York, NY: Guilford.

Holden, R. (1999). Legal implications of sexual assault. In: R.J. Wilson & D. Lagace (Eds.), *Assessment, treatment, & supervision of sex offenders.* Ottawa, ON: Correctional Service of Canada.

Martin's Annual Criminal Code (1999). Aurora, ON: Canada Law Book.

Martinson, R. (1974). What works? Questions and answers about prison reform. *The Public Interest, 35,* 22-54.

Mennonite Central Committee (1996). *Community Reintegration Project Manual.* Toronto, ON: MCC.

Miller, S.B. & Schacter, M. (2000). From restorative justice to restorative governance. *Canadian Journal of Criminology, 42,* 405-420.

Motiuk, L.L. & Brown, S.L. (1996). Factors related to recidivism among released federal sex offenders (*Research Report # R-49*). Ottawa, ON: Research Division, Correctional Service of Canada. (Available at www.csc-scc.gc.ca)

Motiuk, L.L., Belcourt, R.L., & Bonta, J. (1995). Managing high risk offenders: A post detention follow-up (*Research Report #R-39*). Ottawa, ON: Research Branch, Correctional Service of Canada. (available at www.csc-scc.gc.ca)

Quinsey, V.L., Harris, G.T., Rice, M.E., & Cormier, C.A. (1998). *Violent offenders: Appraising and managing risk.* Washington, DC: American Psychological Association.

Roach, K. (2000). Changing punishment at the turn of the century: Restorative justice on the rise. *Canadian Journal of Criminology, 42,* 249-280.

Thurber, A. (1998). Understanding Offender Reintegration. *Forum on Corrections Research, 10.* (available at www.csc-scc.gc.ca)

Wilson, R.J., Kirkegaard, H., & Heise, E. (1998, September). *Community reintegration project for high risk sex offenders.* Presentation at the 23rd Annual Training Institute of the American Probation and Parole Association, Norfolk, VA.

Wilson, R.J., Stewart, L., Stirpe, T., Barrett, M., & Cripps, J.E. (2000). Community-based sex offender management: Combining parole supervision and treatment to reduce recidivism. *Canadian Journal of Criminology, 41,* 177-188.

Treatment of Pedophilia
with Leuprolide Acetate:
A Case Study

Nancy Raymond, MD
Bean Robinson, PhD
Chris Kraft, PhD
Barry Rittberg, MD
Eli Coleman, PhD

SUMMARY. To date, the literature on the treatment of individuals who have committed sexual offenses has focused primarily on psychotherapeutic interventions and the use of antiandrogens. Recently case reports and small series supporting the efficacy of other psychiatric medication, such as serotonin reuptake inhibitors, have been published. Only a few publications have looked at the efficacy of leuprolide acetate, an LH-RH antagonist, in treatment of sex offenders. Leuprolide acetate has advantages

Nancy Raymond is Associate Professor, Department of Psychiatry, and Family Practice and Community Health, and is also Medical Coordinator, Program in Human Sexuality; Bean Robinson and Eli Coleman are members of the faculty, Program in Human Sexuality, Department of Family Practice and Community Health; and Barry Rittberg is Assistant Professor, Department of Psychiatry, University of Minnesota Medical School.

Chris Kraft is Instructor, Department of Psychiatry, Johns Hopkins School of Medicine. He completed this research as a part of his postdoctoral fellowship at the Program in Human Sexuality, University of Minnesota Medical School.

Address correspondence to: Nancy Raymond, Department of Psychiatry, University of Minnesota Medical School, F282/2A West, 2450 Riverside Avenue, Minneapolis, MN 55454 USA (E-mail: raymo002@umn.edu).

[Haworth co-indexing entry note]: "Treatment of Pedophilia with Leuprolide Acetate: A Case Study." Raymond et al. Co-published simultaneously in *Journal of Psychology & Human Sexuality* (The Haworth Press, Inc.) Vol. 13, No. 3/4, 2001, pp. 79-88; and: *Sex Offender Treatment: Accomplishments, Challenges, and Future Directions* (ed: Michael H. Miner, and Eli Coleman) The Haworth Press, Inc., 2001, pp. 79-88. Single or multiple copies of this article are available for a fee from The Haworth Document Delivery Service [1-800-HAWORTH, 9:00 a.m. - 5:00 p.m. (EST). E-mail address: getinfo@haworthpressinc.com].

in terms of less side effects and greater safety during administration when compared to other antiandrogens. In this paper we report on the use of leuprolide acetate in an individual who meets criteria for pedophilia and has multiple other comorbid psychiatric diagnoses. The case report illustrates that leuprolide acetate can be effective in decreasing pedophilic fantasies, urges and behaviors. In addition, individuals who receive effective individualized pharmacotherapeutic treatment for compulsive sexual urges and comorbid psychiatric conditions also respond better to psychotherapeutic interventions. *[Article copies available for a fee from The Haworth Document Delivery Service: 1-800-HAWORTH. E-mail address: <getinfo@haworthpressinc.com> Website: <http://www.HaworthPress.com> © 2001 by The Haworth Press, Inc. All rights reserved.]*

KEYWORDS. LH-RH antagonist, leuprolide acetate, pedophilia, child molesting, antiandrogens

INTRODUCTION

To date, the literature on the treatment of individuals who have committed sexual offenses has focused primarily on psychotherapeutic interventions and the use of antiandrogens. With a few additional reports on the use of other psychiatric medications in terms of pharmacotherapies, the most extensive literature is on the use of antiandrogen medications to treat individuals who have committed sex crimes. Based on the theory that decreasing sexual drive or eliminating the ability to perform sexually will reduce criminal behavior on the part of individuals who have committed a sex offense, various clinicians and researchers have used either medroxy progesterone acetate (MPA) (Cooper, Sandhu, Losztyn, & Cernovsky, 1992; Kiersch, 1990) or cyproterone acetate (CPA) (Bradford & Pawlak, 1987; Cooper, 1987; Cooper & Cernovsky, 1992; Cooper & Cernovsky, 1994; Cooper, Cernovsky, & Magnus, 1992; Cooper, Sandhu et al., 1992) to reduce sexual offenses. Most of these publications have been case reports supporting the efficacy of these medications. There have been a few placebo-controlled studies (e.g., Bradford & Pawlak, 1993; Cooper, 1981; Cooper, Sandhu et al., 1992) which have indicated that treatment with antiandrogens does decrease subjective reports of sexual arousal and sexual interests, as well as leading to a decrease in the frequency of sexual behavior. Cooper, Sandhu et al. (1992) have even reported on a double-blind placebo-controlled trial of MPA and CPA with seven pedophiles. They reported equivalent efficacy for both medications in reducing sexual thoughts and fantasies, reducing the frequency of early morning erection, reducing the frequency and pleasure from masturbation and reducing the level of sexual frustration. However, CPA is not available in the United States, and it has long been recognized by clinicians and researchers alike that MPA has significant sexual side effects, including weight gain, fatigue, nervousness, depressed mood, upset stomach, diarrhea, gynecomastia, thrombophlebitis, hyperglycemia and gall bladder disease.

There are also several case reports and small series which indicate serotonergic reuptake inhibitors (SSRIs) can be efficacious in treating compulsive characteristics of sex offending behavior (Bradford & Gratzer, 1995; Bourgeois & Klein, 1996; Coleman, Cesnik, Moore, & Dwyer, 1992; Emmanuel, Lydiard, & Ballenger, 1991; Kafka, 1991a, 1991b; Kafka, 1994; Kafka & Prentky, 1992; Perilstein, Lipper, & Friedman, 1991; Stein, Hollander, Anthony, Schneier, Fallon, Liebowitz, & Klein,1992). Case reports on the efficacy of tricyclic antidepression (Kafka, 1991a; Snaith & Collins, 1981), buspirone hydrochloride (Federoff, 1998) and lithium (Kafka, 1991a) have been published. There is also a double-blind crossover study that indicates both desipramine and clomipramine are efficacious in treating paraphilias (Kruesi & Fine, 1992).

More recently, case reports have appeared in the literature suggesting the use of leuprolide acetate (Briken, Nika, & Berner, 2001; Cooper & Cernovsky, 1994; Dickey, 1992; Krueger & Kaplan, 2001; Thibaut, 1993, 1996) to reduce levels of circulating androgen in pedophilic and other sex offenders. Leuprolide acetate is a synthetic analog of leutinizing hormone-releasing hormone (LH-RH), which is one of the gonadotropin-releasing hormones (GnRH). Therefore, leuprolide acetate is a potent LH-RH agonist. Initially leuprolide acetate stimulates the release of production of testosterone and other testicular steroids. This can lead to an initial increase in sexual drive, but with chronic administration testicular steroidogenesis is suppressed and sexual drive and function decrease accordingly. Leuprolide acetate has the advantage of relatively fewer side effects. Short-term common side effects include hot flashes, nausea, dizziness. The main concern with long-term use is osteopenia. While side effects, such as gynecomastia, thromboembolism, edema, hepatic toxicity, and gall bladder disease, have been reported with leuprolide acetate, they are much less common than with the other agents.

Below we present the case of a patient who presented for treatment in our outpatient sex offender treatment program on a voluntary basis and elected to try leuprolide acetate after multiple other medications had failed to adequately reduce his pedophilic urges.

CASE STUDY

Presenting Complaint and Psychiatric Diagnoses

The patient was a 41-year-old male who presented voluntarily for treatment in our sex offender treatment program. He presented with great distress and self-hatred about his chronic inability to control his sexual feelings and behaviors toward children. At the time of evaluation, the patient was diagnosed with pedophilia. He exhibited a strong compulsive component to his pedophilic behavior and his overall sexual behavior. He had clear sexual preferences for and arousal to young male children, ages 10-18, but also attractions toward adult males. He began abusing younger boys as an adolescent, often while he was babysitting for them. He continued to have sex with younger boys over the years, encountering them as part of his cruising and exposing behavior. His pattern involved cruising the streets for (preferably) young male prostitutes and using sex phone lines to set up meetings leading to sexual encounters with men and boys. As an adult, he estimated that he has had sexual contact with at least 40 boys, including fondling his young nephew, and developed longer-term sexual relationships with five boys that lasted months or years. His relationships with boys usually involved sex in exchange for gifts, money, trips, rides, etc. Force and coercion were used in the sexual encounters and he found this sexually stimulating. He reported having approximately 800-1,000 adult male sexual partners over the years, many of them anonymous sexual encounters with men he met on the streets, in bookstores, and with male prostitutes. He also reported a history of exhibitionism, frotteurism, and compulsive masturbation since the age of 12. When he began treatment he reported almost constant and unremitting sexual arousal. He reported multiple urges to have sex with minor boys when observing children in public and private settings (e.g., friends of his children, relatives, etc.) as well as chronic urges to cruise for young male prostitutes and vulnerable boys.

He also reported other compulsive behaviors that would be consistent with a diagnosis of an impulse control disorder NOS, such as compulsive gambling (sometimes losing $3,500 in a week), compulsive shopping (he has spent as much as one-third, $50,000, of his retirement in a few months), and shoplifting. At the time of presentation in our outpatient clinic he had a history of substance dependence beginning at 12 years. He had just completed inpatient substance abuse treatment for his amphetamine, marijuana, and cocaine abuse and had been abstinent for one month.

He was also diagnosed with bipolar disorder, rapid cycling type. Treating and monitoring these comorbid conditions was seen as an integral part of the treatment of his sexual disorder.

Psychotherapeutic Treatment

The patient was treated for eight months in our intensive, comprehensive outpatient, sex offender treatment program. Treatment focused on stopping offending behavior by identifying, setting up and adhering to behavioral boundaries and avoiding risk situations, abstaining from mood altering substances, developing and understanding the sexual offense cycle, minimizing denial and taking responsibility for offending behavior, developing empathy for victims, development of diverse family and social support systems that are actively involved in both treatment and social activities, and, finally, developing healthy and appropriate sexual behavior. Frequency of treatment consisted of weekly two-hour group psychotherapy sessions with other sexual offenders; twice monthly family or individual psychotherapy sessions with family, friends, and support persons, including other group members; and monthly outpatient psychiatric medication management.

Pharmacologic Treatment

He was initially treated with combinations of valproic acid and lithium carbonate in an attempt to stabilize his bipolar mood disorder. The patient was quite sensitive to the sedative side effects of both and did not tolerate therapeutic levels of either medication well. Concurrently, he was treated with venlafaxine, 150 to 225 mg once a day, to treat depressive symptoms and in the hope that the serotonergic effects might decrease his compulsive sexual preoccupations. The patient was able to exercise good control over his behavior much of this time. However, he continued to report an almost-constant preoccupation with fantasies regarding having sex with young boys.

Subsequently, due to worsening of depression, and a marked increase in suicidal ideation, strong urges to use cocaine and to act out sexually, the patient was admitted to the hospital. During this hospitalization, his bipolar symptoms were stabilized on a combination of gabapentin 300 mg three times per day and valproic acid sprinkles 125 mg, six capsules per day (dosed in this fashion to prevent sedative side effects). The venlafaxine that he had been taking prior to admission was discontinued and paroxotine was tried, thinking that the sexual side effects of paroxotine might help control his sexual urges. However, the patient found that the delayed ejaculation caused by the paroxetine actually caused an increase in pedophilic fantasies because even more intense fantasies were required in order for him to have orgasm during masturbation.

The addition of leuprolide acetate to his current medication and psychotherapeutic regimen was discussed with the patient. He was informed of possible side effects, including a decrease in sexual function, decreased libido, and a decrease in bone mineral density. He was also informed that its use in men to treat pedophilia was not an FDA approved indication for the medication. The patient, however, described himself as desperate to have some relief from pedophilic fantasies and urges and consented to take the medication. The patient was given a test dose of 1.0 mg subcutaneously. The next day he received his first intramuscular dose of 7.5 mg of leuprolide acetate intramuscularly (IM). He was discharged on 7.5 mg IM every month. Because our mental health clinic did not have the facilities to administer IM injections, an arrangement was made with his internist's office to have a nurse administer the medication and fax documentation to us on a monthly basis. Within seven to ten days he reported a decrease in pedophilic fantasies. Within one to two months after his discharge from the hospital, he reported a dramatic reduction in his pedophilic urges (from incessant daily urges to 1-7 urges a week) and a dramatic reduction from his constant preoccupation with pedophilic fantasies. He reported that he was no longer cruising the streets looking for young male prostitutes.

Three months after discharge from the hospital, the patient reported hypomanic symptoms, including elevated mood, pressured speech, increased productive activity, racing thoughts, and an increase in preoccupation with pedophilic fantasies. However, he reported no acting on urges and no cruising behavior. Gabapentin was increased to 1200 mg three times per day in response to this exacerbation of manic symptomatology. Other medications remained unchanged.

During the first six months after hospital discharge with continued administration of leuprolide acetate, the patient reported a marked decrease in pedophilic fantasies and urges to act out. He was not cruising to find sexual partners and he engaged in other high-risk behaviors only two to three times per month instead of several times per week, as he had prior to treatment with leuprolide. This was followed by a six-month period during which, for the first time, the patient reported being free of such pedophilic urges. Initially, he reported no problems with masturbation when he chose to, but a marked decrease in frequency of masturbation. However, four to six months after hospital discharge the patient experienced a loss of sexual function to the point that masturbation became painful and orgasm nearly impossible. The decision was made to reduce the dose of leuprolide acetate to see if sexual function could be improved without a recurrence of urges to offend. Particularly since this patient was in sex offender treatment voluntarily, patient satisfaction was necessary to insure compliance with the regimen. The dose of leuprolide acetate was adjusted to 5.0 mg IM every month. Patient now reports masturbation and consensual sexual relations are possible, but he has also seen an increase in fantasies and interest in sexual behavior with children over the six months he has been on this dose. He has some increase in urges to approach children but has not acted on them and he is not cruising. However, we will continue to monitor and titrate the leuprolide acetate dose in response to both sexual functioning and pedophilic fantasies and urges.

DISCUSSION

This case illustrates a challenging instance of an individual with pedophilia and numerous comorbid diagnoses which necessitated the use of pharmacotherapy in combination with specialized psychological sex offender treatment. It adds to the case reports illustrating the effectiveness of leuprolide acetate, but it also illustrates how it might be combined with other pharmacotherapies given the complexity of a patient's psychiatric difficulties. While mono-pharmacotherapy may be effective as a first line response in the treatment of sexual offenders, the astute clinician will consider a combination of pharmacotherapies to control a variety of comorbid psychiatric conditions.

In this case the patient has been willing to accept the side effects and risks of leuprolide acetate because of the benefits he sees in the reduction of his constant preoccupation with pursuing sexual relations with children. Our research group has adopted a model in which patients who have presentations similar to this would be categorized as suffering from what Coleman (1991, 1992) has identified as paraphilic compulsive sexual behavior. In our clinical experience, and based on multiple case reports (cited previously), serotonin reuptake inhibitors and other medications that affect the serotonin system have been found to be efficacious in treating individuals with paraphilic and non-paraphilic compulsive sexual behavior. This case illustrates that leuprolide acetate may be a useful adjunct in the treatment of individuals with severe paraphilic compulsive sexual behavior if other methods have failed. Clinically, the primary advantage of leuprolide acetate over MPA or CPA is the markedly reduced incidence of side effects.

Certainly when the patient is taking such a medication voluntarily it is important to try to titrate the dose to allow for some sexual function in order to increase continued medication compliance. Close coordination between medical staff and therapists is essential to the outpatient management of patients such as this in order to ensure that all providers have the same information regarding level of symptoms and the treatment plan. Care of patients with pedophilia puts the provider at significant medical legal risk unless the care is provided through a comprehensive treatment program.

Concurrent psychotherapy is always indicated in the treatment of these patients. No one is advocating that medication alone is effective in this population. Of note, psychotherapy for the patient's sexual offending was more productive once his unremitting/constant pedophilic fantasies and urges were better controlled. Prior to effective pharmacological management of these fantasies and urges psychotherapy was, of necessity, focused on crisis management in order to control his inappropriate sexual urges and behaviors. Once this behavioral control was obtained, we were able to focus on other psychotherapeutic areas such as:

1. involving his children, brother and other family and friends in treatment;
2. using additional strategies to help him cope with his severe bipolar illness;
3. helping him control his urges to gamble, shop, shoplift, and use chemicals; and
4. making some long overdue career changes, to name a few of the more prominent issues.

Further controlled trials are needed to determine the efficacy of leuprolide acetate in the treatment of pedophilia. Additional studies also are needed to determine if concurrent psychotherapy and individu-ally-tailored pharmacotherapy may lead to more effective treatment of individuals who have committed sexual offenses. In the meantime, cli-nicians will need to be guided by the extant clinical case study literature. This will necessitate greater involvement of psychiatrists knowledgeable in treating paraphilias as well as the typical array of psychiatric disor-ders present in the sexual offender treatment programs. This will also require more specialized training of psychiatrists who rarely receive this type of specialized instruction as part of their residency program.

REFERENCES

Bourgeois, J.A., & Klein, M. (1996). Risperidone and fluoxetine in the treatment of pedophilia with comorbid dysthymia [letter to the editor]. *Journal of Clinical Psychopharmacology, 16*(3), 257-258.

Bradford, J.M.W., & Gratzer, T.G. (1995). A treatment for impulse control disorders and paraphilia: A case report. *Canadian Journal of Psychiatry, 40*, 4-5.

Bradford, J.McD.W., & Pawlak, A. (1987). Sadistic homosexual pedophilia: Treat-ment with cyproterone acetate: A single case study. *Canadian Journal of Psychia-try, 32*, 22-30.

Bradford, J.M., & Pawlak, A. (1993). Double-blind placebo crossover study of cyproterone acetate in the treatment of the paraphilias. *Archives of Sexual Behavior, 22*(5), 383-402.

Briken, P., Nika, E., & Berner, W. (2001). Treatment of paraphilia with leutinizing hormone-releasing agonists. *Journal of Sex & Marital Therapy, 27*(1), 45-55.

Coleman, E. (1991). Compulsive sexual behavior: New concepts and treatments. *Jour-nal of the Psychology of Human Sexuality, 4*, 37-52.

Coleman, E. (1992). Is your patient suffering from compulsive sexual behavior? *Psy-chiatric Annals, 22*, 320-325.

Coleman, E., Cesnik, J., Moore, A.M., & Dwyer, S.M. (1992). An exploratory study of the role of psychotropic medications in the treatment of sex offenders. *Journal of Offender Rehabilitation, 18*(3/4), 75-88.

Cooper, A.J. (1981). A placebo-controlled trial of the antiandrogen cyproterone ace-tate in deviant hypersexuality. *Comprehensive Psychiatry, 22*(5), 458-465.

Cooper, A.J. (1987). Sadistic homosexual pedophilia treatment with cyproterone ace-tate. *Canadian Journal of Psychiatry, 32*(8), 738-740.

Cooper, A.J., & Cernovsky, Z. (1992). The effects of cyproterone acetate on sleeping and waking penile erections in pedophiles: Possible implications for treatment. *Ca-nadian Journal of Psychiatry, 37*, 33-39.

Cooper, A.J., & Cernovsky, Z.Z. (1994). Comparison of cyproterone acetate (CPA) and leuprolide acetate (LHRH agonist) in a chronic pedophile: A clinical case study. *Society of Biological Psychiatry, 36*, 269-271.

Cooper, A.J., Cernovsky, Z., & Magnus, R.V. (1992). The long term use of cyproterone acetate in pedophilia: A case study. *Journal of Sex and Marital Therapy, 18*(4), 292-302.

Cooper, A.J., Sandhu, S., Losztyn, S., & Cernovsky, Z. (1992). A double-blind placebo controlled trial of medroxyprogesterone acetate and cyproterone acetate with seven pedophiles. *Canadian Journal of Psychiatry, 37*, 687-693.

Dickey, R. (1992). The management of a case of treatment-resistant paraphilia with a long-acting LHRH agonist. *Canadian Journal of Psychiatry, 37*, 567-569.

Emmanuel, N.P., Lydiard, R.B., & Ballenger, J.C. (1991). Fluoxetine treatment of voyeurism. *American Journal of Psychiatry, 148*(7), 950.

Federoff, J.P. (1988). Buspirone hydrochloride in the treatment of transvestic fetishism. *Journal of Clinical Psychiatry, 49*(10), 408-409.

Kafka, M.P. (1991a). Successful antidepressant treatment of nonparaphilic sexual addictions and paraphilias in men. *Journal of Clinical Psychiatry, 52*(2), 60-65.

Kafka, M.P. (1991b). Successful treatment of paraphilic coercive disorder (a rapist) with fluoxetine hydrochloride. *British Journal of Psychiatry, 158*, 844-847.

Kafka, M.P. (1994). Sertraline pharmacotherapy for paraphilias and paraphilia-related disorders: An open trial. *Annals of Clinical Psychiatry, 6*(3), 189-195.

Kafka, M.P., & Prentky, R. (1992). Fluoxetine treatment of nonparaphilic sexual addictions and paraphilias in men. *Journal of Clinical Psychiatry, 53*(10), 351-358.

Kiersch, T.A. (1990). Treatment of sex offenders with depo-provera. *Bulletin of the American Academy of Psychiatry & Law, 18*(2), 179-187.

Krueger, R.B., & Kaplan, M.S. (2001). Depot-leuprolide acetate for treatment of paraphilias: A report of twelve cases. *Archives of Sexual Behavior, 30*(4), 409-422.

Kruesi, A.J., & Fine, S. (1992). Paraphilias: A double-blind crossover comparison of Climipramine versus Desipramine. *Archives of Sexual Behavior, 21*(6), 587-593.

Perilstein, R.D., Lipper, S., & Friedman, L.J. (1991). Three cases of paraphilias responsive to fluoxetine treatment. *Journal of Clinical Psychiatry, 52*(4), 169-170.

Snaith, R.P., & Collins, S.A. (1981). Five exhibitionists and a method of treatment. *British Journal of Psychiatry, 138*, 126-130.

Stein, D.J., Hollander, E., Anthony, D.T., Schneier, F.R., Fallon, B.A., Liebowitz, M.R., & Klein, D.F. (1992). Serotonergic medications for sexual obsessions, sexual addictions, and paraphilias. *Journal of Clinical Psychiatry, 53*(8), 267-271.

Thibaut, F., Cordier, B., & Kuhn, J.M. (1993). Effect of a long-lasting gonadotrophin hormone-releasing hormone agonist in six cases of severe male paraphilia. *Acta Psychiatrica Scandinavica, 87*, 445-450.

Thibaut, F., Cordier, B., & Kuhn, J.M. (1996). Gonadotrophin hormone releasing hormone agonist in cases of severe paraphilia: A lifetime treatment? *Psychoneuroendocrinology, 21*(4), 411-419.

A Comparison Between Exclusively Male Target and Female/Both Sexes Target Child Molesters on Psychometric Variables, DSM-IV Diagnoses and MTC:CM3 Typology

Reinhard Eher, MD
Christine Gruenhut, MD
Stefan Fruehwald, MD
Patrick Frottier, MD
Brigitte Hobl, MD
Martin Aigner, MD

SUMMARY. Forty-eight men incarcerated for child molestation were divided into two groups on the basis of the gender of their victims: (1) exclusively male target and (2) female or both sexes target child molesters.

Reinhard Eher is affiliated with the Federal Assessment and Documentation Centre for Sexual Offenders in Austria, Vienna, and the Interpersonal Violence Research Centre, Vienna, Austria. Christine Gruenhut, Stefan Fruehwald, Patrick Frottier, Brigitte Hobl and Martin Aigner are affiliated with the Department of Social Psychiatry, University Medical School Vienna and Justizanstalt Wien-Mittersteig, Vienna, Austria.

Address correspondence to: Reinhard Eher, Federal Assessment and Documentation Centre for Sexual Offenders in Austria, Justizanstalt Wien-Mittersteig, Aussenstelle Floridsdorf, Gerichtsgasse 6, A-1210 Vienna, Austria (E-mail: reinhard. eher@univie. ac.at).

This research was supported by a grant from the Austrian National Bank (Project Nr. 6479).

[Haworth co-indexing entry note]: "A Comparison Between Exclusively Male Target and Female/Both Sexes Target Child Molesters on Psychometric Variables, DSM-IV Diagnoses and MTC:CM3 Typology." Eher et al. Co-published simultaneously in *Journal of Psychology & Human Sexuality* (The Haworth Press, Inc.) Vol. 13, No. 3/4, 2001, pp. 89-102; and: *Sex Offender Treatment: Accomplishments, Challenges, and Future Directions* (ed: Michael H. Miner, and Eli Coleman) The Haworth Press, Inc., 2001, pp. 89-102. Single or multiple copies of this article are available for a fee from The Haworth Document Delivery Service [1-800-HAWORTH, 9:00 a.m. - 5:00 p.m. (EST). E-mail address: getinfo@haworthpressinc.com].

Psychiatric co-morbidity was measured using the Structured Clinical Interview for DSM-IV. Offenders were described in terms of the MTC:CM3 child molester typology, and they completed self-report instruments that measured aggressiveness, anger, depression, anxiety, and social anxiety. Psychiatric co-morbidity did not differ significantly across groups except for the prevalence of alcohol abuse/dependence, which was found to be significantly higher in the female/mixed gender target group. No differences were found on measures of aggressiveness, anger, depression, anxiety, or social anxiety. However, exclusively male target offenders were found to be less socially competent and to be high in contact with children on the MTC:CM3 typology. These data may provide evidence to confirm previous findings that male target child molesters are at higher risk for re-offending. *[Article copies available for a fee from The Haworth Document Delivery Service: 1-800-HAWORTH. E-mail address: <getinfo@haworthpressinc.com> Website: <http://www.HaworthPress.com> © 2001 by The Haworth Press, Inc. All rights reserved.]*

KEYWORDS. Child molesters, psychiatric co-morbidity, victim sex, offender typology

The gender of the victims of child molesters has long been thought to be an important factor in determining the differences between risk for re-offense and the etiology of sex crimes. As early as 1957, Radzinowicz (1957) reported that a typological distinction based on the sex of the victim of child molesters was successful in predicting recidivism. Child molesters whose index offense was against girls had a 13% reconviction rate for a new sexual offense whereas male target child molesters were reconvicted at a rate of 27% after four years. Fitch (1962) and Frisbie and Dondis (1965) also reported higher re-offense rates for men who molested boys when compared to those with female victims. Fitch (1962) concluded that recidivists were more likely to be male target offenders, to have more previous convictions for sexual offenses, and to have been convicted of their first sexual offense at a younger age. Sturgeon and Taylor (1980) reported an 18% reconviction rate for child molesters who had offended against females and 38% for male target child molesters in a prison cohort. They also found male target child molesters had more prior convictions for both sexual and non-sexual offenses. Quinsey et al. (1995), in a review of follow-up studies, reported that the average sexual reconviction rate for female target child molesters was 18%, and, for male target samples, the reconviction rate was 35%.

A major weakness of these studies is that they grouped subjects on the basis of the victims' gender for the index offense. They did not include the victims of any prior offenses, and they also did not include offenders who had offended against both boys and girls. Hanson et al. (1993), who divided subjects into offenders who had molested boys only, girls only and children of both genders, found that it was the "boys only" variable that significantly correlated with sexual recidivism.

The differential reconviction rates based on the gender-of-victim distinction has not received consistent support. Marshall and Barbaree (1988) followed up 35 extrafamilial sex offenders against victims under age 16. Their data did not indicate a difference in the reconviction rate between female and male targeting offenders over a four-year follow-up period. Moreover, Prentky et al. (1997) followed up 111 child molesters with times at risk between 11 and 25 years. They also found that gender of victim did not influence recidivism rates.

Despite the above evidence that victim gender in child molesters may be important to re-offending potential, there have been few studies that have explored the differences between male target and female target child molesters on typological variables or psychiatric co-morbidity. The results of the studies cited above may be due to differences between child molesters offending against boys and girls with respect to psychiatric co-morbidity. It is also possible that the victim gender dichotomy may actually be accounted for by typology variables such as fixation and social competence.

Prentky et al. (1997) presented a study examining the predictive efficacy of variables derived from the MTC:CM3 typology (Knight, 1989; Prentky et al., 1989; Knight et al., 1989). The "fixation" variable (degree of sexual preoccupation with children), the existence of paraphilias and the number of previous sexual offenses predicted sexual recidivism in their sample. However, as stated before, gender of victim did not significantly predict recidivism in this study. These data may indicate that it is differences accounted for by the MTC:CM3 typology that confer differential risk in same and opposite sex child molesters, rather than victim gender per se.

The present study is designed to explore factors that might account for the differential re-offense risk in offenders who offend against male and/or female children. We have compared two groups of offenders, those with only male victims and those with female victims (some of whom also have male victims). This study explores the differences between these groups on the MTC:CM3 typology, psychiatric co-morbidity, and measures of anger, anxiety, depression and interpersonal skills. These findings might be useful for understanding differential re-offense risk, individualising treatment within sex offender treatment programs, and in appropriate use of medication.

METHOD

Participants

The population studied was comprised of forty-eight (48) extrafamilial adult male child molesters imprisoned at the medium security institution, Justizanstalt Wien-Mittersteig in Vienna, Austria. All offenders were defined as mentally ill, although they were not determined to be not guilty for reasons of insanity. The mean age of the sample was 37.7 years. On average, the number of prior sexual offenses against minors and prior nonsexual violent offenses in this group of offenders was 0.9. The average number of prior nonviolent offenses, that is, offenses against property, was 2.3 (Table 1).

Since the "boys-only" variable, but not the "girls only" nor the "boys and girls" variable, was shown to correlate with sexual recidivism in previous research (Hanson et al., 1993), child molesters were divided into two groups: those who had offended against boys only (n = 18) and those who had offended against girls or against children of both genders (n = 30). Subjects were grouped by the gender of victims not only for index offenses but for all prior sexual offenses.

Sources for Data Acquisition

There were three sources of data for this study: clinical interviews of the offenders, prison records, and official records kept by the Ministry of Internal Affairs in Austria. File ratings and interviews were conducted by two research assistants (second and third author) who were blind to the hypothesized relationships amongst the variables. Discrepancies between the ratings were resolved by a consensus of the two raters with the help of the first author. Offense data were analyzed and classified according to Hall (1988) and Hall and Proctor (1987). Thus, offenses included sexual felonies against adults, sexual felonies against children, nonsexual violent offenses (involving actual or threatened harm) and nonviolent offenses against property. All arrests, rearrests, and convictions were recorded.

TABLE 1. Victim Sex and Child Molester Relapse

Radzinowicz (1957) « Cambridge Study »	After 4 years 20% were reconvicted of a sexual offense - *female target CHM: 13% reconviction rate* - *male target CHM: 27% reconviction rate*
Fitch (1962)	1-9 years after prison release - *female target CHM: 13% reconviction rate for sexual offenses* - *male target CHM: 40% reconviction rate for sexual offenses* recidivists were more likely 1. to be homosexual 2. to have more previous convictions for sexual offenses 3. to be younger at conviction for the first sexual offense
Frisbie and Dondis (1965)	After 6 years: - *female target CHM: 22% reconviction rate for sexual offenses* - *male target CHM: 35% reconviction rate for sexual offenses* the recidivism rate for male and female target offenders was similar to that of the female target offenders
Sturgeon and Taylor (1980)	The Prison Cohort: Rate of prior convictions for sexual crimes: - female target CHM: 36% - male target CHM: 69% rate for prior convictions for nonsexual crimes against persons: - female target CHM: 7% - male target CHM: 13% Reconviction Rate: - *female target CHM: 38%* - *male target CHM: 18%*
Barbaree and Marshall (1988)	Follow up of 35 extrafamilial sex offenders against victims under age 16: - 43% reconviction rate during a 4-year follow-up, *no difference between female and male target offenders*
Quinsey et al. (1995)	- weighted average sexual reconviction rate for *female target samples (n = 1,167) was 18.3%* - weighted average sexual reconviction rate for *male target samples (n = 561) was 35.2%*
Hanson et al. (1993)	10- to 31-year follow up of 197 child molesters - **"Boys only–Variable"** significantly correlated with *recidivism (r = 0.24***)*
Prentky et al. (1997)	Follow up of 111 child molesters (11-25 years follow up) - *sex of victim did not influence recidivism rate*

Child Molester Typology (MTC:CM3)

Participants were categorized using the MTC:CM3 typology, which was developed and described extensively by Knight (1989), Prentky et al. (1989) and Knight et al. (1989). The MTC:CM3 is comprised of two independent axes. Axis I requires two dichotomous decisions: the degree of fixation on children and the level of social competence. Degree of fixation on children is defined by number of sexual contacts with children, development of relationships with children and contact with children across situations. Level of social competence is defined by a single job lasting three or more years, a sexual or nonsexual relationship with an adult for at least one year, and significant responsibility in parenting a child. Axis II involves a distinction between offenders exhibiting high and low amount of contact with children. High-contact offenders are subsequently divided into those who seek to establish a relationship with the children (interpersonal type) and those whose contact is exclusively sexually motivated (narcissistic type). Low-contact offenders are subsequently divided according to the degree of physical injury caused during sexual offending and the presence or absence of sexual sadism.

Psychiatric Co-Morbidity

All subjects were interviewed by one of the authors using a German version of the Structured Clinical Interview for DSM-IV (SCID). The SCID has two versions, the SCID I (Wittchen et al., 1997), which provides diagnoses of Axis I disorders, and the SCID II (Fydrich et al., 1997), which provides diagnoses of Axis II disorders. The SCID I does not include a section for diagnosis of psychosexual disorders, nor is another standardized structured interview available to make such diagnoses. Therefore, diagnoses of sexual disorders were done according to criteria set forth in the DSM-IV (APA, 1994).

Psychometric Measures

Assessment of Factors of Aggressiveness (FAF: Hampel & Selg, 1975). The FAF was used to measure aggressiveness. It is similar to the American Buss-Durkee Hostility Inventory (Buss & Durkee, 1957) and includes items related to hostility, including the following subscales: spontaneous aggression, reactive aggression, and self-aggression.

State-Trait Anxiety Inventory (STAI: Spielberger et al., 1970). The STAI is a self-report measure of current anxious mood (state) and general level of anxiety (trait).

State Trait Anger Inventory (Schwenkmezger et al., 1992) is a measure of anger that includes emotional and behavioral aspects of anger. It includes the following scales: state anger, trait anger, inward directed anger, outward directed anger, and anger control.

Beck Depression Inventory (Hautzinger et al., 1991) is a 20-item self-report instrument that measures current symptoms of depression.

Social Interaction Anxiety (SIAS: Stangier et al., 1997). Measures social anxiety in interactions with other people.

Social Phobia (SPS: Stangier et al., 1997). Measures social anxiety in situations where one can be observed but is not necessarily interacting with other people.

RESULTS

MTC:CM3 Typology and Criminology

Table 2 presents the results of categorizing this sample using the MCT:CM3 typology. Eighty-one percent of the total sample were found to meet criteria for high fixation using the MCT:CM3 criteria. Those offenders high on fixation were also found to meet DSM-IV criteria for pedophilia (Table 2). About sixty percent (60.4%) of the sample were high on the social competence scale and 65% spent a substantial amount of their time in close proximity to children, thus meeting the MTC:CM3 "high contact" criterion (Table 2). Out of the "high contact" group, 37.5% represented the "interpersonal" type, and 27.1% the narcissistic type. Of those who had been rated as "low contact" child molesters, 14.6% were categorized as "exploitative," 6.3% as "muted sadistic," 10.4% as "aggressive," and 4.2% as "overt sadistic."

T-test analyses showed that the mean age of child molesters who had offended against girls only or against children of both sexes (41.8 years) was significantly higher than that for male target offenders (30.8 years). Also, male target child molesters were found to have a significantly lower age of first conviction than female targeting/mixed offenders (Table 3). Nevertheless, the conviction rates for prior sexual and nonsexual violent offenses were similar in both groups (see Table 3). Child molesters offending against girls only or against children of both sexes, on the other hand, showed a higher rate for property offenses (Table 3).

TABLE 2. Criminology and MTC:CM3 Typology (n = 48)

Age	37.7
Prior sexual offenses against minors	0.94
Prior nonsexual violent offenses	0.97
Prior offenses against property	2.28
MTC:CM3 – Typology AXIS I	
High fixation	39 (81.3%)
High social competence	29 (60.4%)
AXIS II *1. high amount of contact*	
type 1: Interpersonal	18 (37.5%)
type 2: Narcissistic	13 (27.1%)
2. low amount of contact	
type 3: low physical injury, low sadism ("exploitative")	7 (14.6%)
type 4: low physical injury, high sadism ("muted sadistic")	3 (6.3%)
type 5: high physical injury, low sadism ("aggressive")	5 (10.4%)
type 6: high physical injury, high sadism ("overt sadistic")	2 (4.2%)

Chi-square analyses revealed that the male target offenders were found to be lower in social competence. Only seven, compared to 22 of those with female victims, could be assigned to the "highly socially competent" type according to MTC:CM3 criteria (Table 3). Also, the male target offenders were found to spend more time in close proximity to children in both sexual and non-sexual situations, thus they were defined as "high contact." The "interpersonal" and "narcissistic" type were seen more often in the male target offenders than in those with female victims. No male target offenders were categorized as the "exploitative" type, whereas 23% of those offenders with female victims were categorized as "exploitative." No difference across groups were found in the "muted sadistic," "aggressive" or "overt sadistic" types.

Psychiatric Co-Morbidity

The only significant difference found between offender groups was the lifetime prevalence of alcohol abuse/dependence (see Table 4). Half of the offenders targeting girls only or children of both sexes had a lifetime diagnosis of alcohol abuse or dependence, whereas only one quarter of the exclusively male target offenders had an equivalent diagnosis.

TABLE 3. Comparison Between Female and Both Sexes Target Child Molesters and Exclusively Male Target Child Molesters (Criminology and MTC:CM3 Typology)

	Female and both sexes target offenders (n = 30)	Exclusively male target offenders (n = 18)
Age	41.8	30.8***
Age at first conviction	25.9	22.2*
Prior sexual offenses against minors	0.9	1.0
Prior nonsexual violent offenses	0.9	1.1
Prior offenses against property	2.7	1.8
MTC:CM3 – Typology		
AXIS I		
High fixation	24 (80%)	15 (83.3%)
High social competence	22 (73.3%)	7 (39%)***
AXIS II		
1. high amount of contact		
type 1: Interpersonal	10 (33.3%)	8 (44.4%)*
type 2: Narcissistic	7 (23.3%)	6 (33.3%)*
2. low amount of contact		
type 3: low physical injury, low sadism ("exploitative")	7 (23.3%)	0**
type 4: low physical injury, high sadism ("muted sadistic")	2 (6.7%)	1 (5.6%)
type 5: high physical injury, low sadism ("aggressive")	3 (10%)	2 (11.1%)
type 6: high physical injury, high sadism ("overt sadistic")	1 (3.3%)	1 (5.6%)

* $p < 0.05$, ** $p < 0.01$, ***$p < .001$ (T-Test, Chi-Square)

There were no other significant differences between groups on other Axis I or Axis II mental disorders.

Psychometric Measures

No significant differences were found between offender groups on any of the psychometric measures of aggressiveness, anger, anxiety, social anxiety or depression (see Table 5).

TABLE 4. Comparison Between Female and Both Sexes Target Child Molesters and Exclusively Male Target Child Molesters (Psychiatric Co-Morbidity)

DSM-IV Diagnoses in %	Female and both sexes target offenders (n = 30)	Exclusively male target offenders (n = 18)
Affective disorders	7 (23.3%)	2 (11.1%)
Alcohol abuse or dependence	14 (46.7%)	5 (28%)**
Substance abuse/dependence	4 (13.3%)	1 (5.6%)
Anxiety disorders	3 (10%)	1 (5.6%)
Sexual sadism/masochism	3 (10%)	2 (11%)
Fetishism/transvestitic fetishism	0	1 (5.6%)
Voyeurism	0	1 (5.6%)
Exhibitionism	2 (6.7%)	1 (5.6%)
Avoidant PD	6 (20%)	3 (16.7%)
Dependent PD	0	0
OC PD	0	0
Paranoid PD	0	1 (5.6%)
Schizotypal PD	0	1 (5.6%)
Schizoid PD	0	0
Histrionic PD	0	0
Narcissistic PD	2 (6.7%)	3 (16.7%)
Borderline PD	2 (6.7%)	2 (11.1%)
Antisocial PD	5 (16.7%)	4 (22.2%)

**$p < 0.01$ (Chi-Square)

DISCUSSION

Although the division of child molesters on the basis of the victim gender was one of the earliest empirical discriminators, so far no comparison between male and female target child molesters has been undertaken in terms of psychiatric co-morbidity and offender typology. In our study we divided 48 child molesters into two groups on the basis of whether they had ever offended against female children (and maybe additionally against boys) or exclusively against male minors. The empirical basis for this distinction was the work of Hanson et al. (1993) finding out that the "boys only" variable significantly contributed to sexual recidivism. In each group about 80% could be found to meet

TABLE 5. Comparison Between Female and Both Sexes Target Child Molesters and Exclusively Male Target Child Molesters

Psychometric measures	Female and both sexes target offenders (n = 30)	Exclusively male target offenders (n = 18)
Aggressiveness (FAF)		
- spontaneous aggression	3.6	3.1
- reactive aggression	3.1	2.8
- self aggression	5.3	5.2
Anger (STAXI)		
- state anger	14.1	14.8
- trait anger	16.7	15.6
- anger outward directed	11.0	11.2
- anger control	24.7	23.4
Anxiety (STAI)		
- state anxiety	44.1	41.4
- trait anxiety	40.4	38.8
Depression (BDI)	16.3	15.8
Social Anxiety		
- Social Interaction Anxiety (SIAS)	21.4	18.9
- Social Phobia (SPS)	12.4	11.2

DSM-IV criteria for pedophilia and to be high on the MTC:CM3 fixation criterion. Offenders who had exclusively transgressed males turned out to be significantly less socially competent according to MTC:CM3 criteria. That means that those offenders had fewer peer relationships with adults and that they were less likely to have had a permanent job (Knight et al., 1989). Also, the proportion of those who spent substantial time in close proximity to children in sexual and non-sexual situations was higher ("high contact") in the male target group. Exclusively male targeting offenders were found to be significantly younger and to be convicted for their first time significantly earlier than offenders who exclusively or additionally transgressed females. Also, during an artificial "exposure time" (time from first conviction until our investigation) male target offenders were found to have the same offense rates as those targeting females although exposure time was 16 years for female/mixed target offenders compared to eight years for male target offenders.

These findings may help explain the higher reconviction rates in male target child molesters found in previous studies (Radzinowicz, 1957; Fitch, 1962; Frisbie & Dondies, 1965; Sturgeon & Taylor, 1980). Lower social competence and more contact with children, even in non-sexual contexts, might be one explanation for the higher reconviction rates. It may also be that child molestation in combination with homosexuality is viewed as more abnormal than heterosexual child molestation, where one could argue that "only" the age of the "partner" was wrong. This may provide a better basis for minimizing and justifying the offense.

We were not able to find possible explanations for this different conviction rate by psychiatric co-morbidity or psychometric measures. The only difference was found in the lifetime prevalence of alcohol abuse and dependence. In male target offenders only 28% reported the existence of problems with alcohol, whereas about 50% of the female/mixed target offenders had a diagnosis of alcohol abuse or dependence. The prevalence of affective disorder, anxiety disorders, paraphilias and personality disorders did not differ significantly. In general, our findings concerning psychiatric co-morbidity were much different from those found by Raymond et al. (1999). In our study we found lower rates of psychiatric co-morbidity in all DSM-IV sections except for alcohol problems. This might be a consequence of different populations studied: whereas our investigation was done with a forensic inpatient population of offenders who were judged to be mentally ill although guilty, Raymond et al. (1999) interviewed offenders mainly from outpatient treatment programs. Also, incarcerated offenders like our sample, although supposed to exhibit higher psychiatric co-morbidity, may deny psychiatric symptoms since they knew that mental illness was one reason to be detained in custody.

Summarizing our findings one has to critically take into account the low sample size, especially for male target offenders. This limitation on statistical power may account for some of the failure to replicate differences between groups found in previous literature. This also limits the generalizability of our results, although we did find some results that were consistent with prior studies. Psychiatric co-morbidity studies should be repeated with random samples corrected for age and total numbers of prior convictions. Nevertheless, from a clinical point of view, our results are interesting: twice as many male target offenders were found to be socially incompetent according to MTC:CM3 typology criteria underlining the importance of including male target offenders in social competence trainings. Nearly 80% of male target offenders compared to 50% in the female/mixed group could be shown to look for a high amount of contact to children. High amount of contact is negatively correlated to violent re-offense (Prentky et al., 1997). Being higher on risk for re-offense but lower on risk for violent re-offense and also lower on risk for substance abuse may indicate that outpatient programs, including control mechanisms, may be an appropriate recommendation for male target offenders who do not have an antisocial personality disorder. It may be less efficient and cost-effective to detain these offenders in custody.

REFERENCES

Barbaree H., & Marshall W. (1988). Deviant sexual arousal, offense history, and demographic variables as predictors of reoffense among child molester. *Behavior Science and the Law, 6*, 267-280.

Buss, A.H., & Durkee, A. (1957). An inventory for assessing different kinds of hostility. *Journal of Consulting and Clinical Psychology, 21*, 343-348.

Fitch, J.H. (1962). Men convicted of sexual offenses against children: A descriptive follow-up study. *British Journal of Criminology, 3*, 18-37.

Frisbie, L.V., & Dondis, E.H. (1965). *Recidivism among treated sex offenders* (California Mental Health Research Monograph No. 5). State of California Department of Mental Hygiene, Los Angeles.

Fydrich, T., Renneber, B., Schmitz, B., & Wittchen, H.-U. (1997). *SKID-II. Strukturiertes Klinisches Interview für DSM-IV Achse II: Persönlichkeitsstörungen.* Göttingen: Hogrefe.

Hall, G.C.N. (1988). Criminal behavior as a function of clinical and actuarial variables in a sexual offender population. *Journal of Consulting and Clinical Psychology, 56*, 773-775.

Hall, G.C.N., & Proctor, W.C. (1987). Criminological predictors of recidivism in a sexual offender population. *Journal of Consulting and Clinical Psychology, 55*, 111-112.

Hampel, R., & Selg, H. (1975). *FAF- Fragebogen zur Erfassung von Aggressivitätsfaktoren (FAF–Inventory for the Assessment of Factors of Aggressiveness).* Göettingen: Hogrefe.

Hanson, R.K., Steffy, R.A., & Gauthier, R. (1993). Long-term recidivism of child molesters. *Journal of Consulting and Clinical Psychology, 61*, 646-652.

Hautzinger, M., Beiler, M., & Worall, H. (1991). *Das Beck-Depressionsinventar–(BDI).* Bern: Huber.

Knight, R.A. (1989). An assessment of the concurrent validity of a child molester typology. *Journal of Interpersonal Violence, 4*, 131-150.

Knight, R.A., Carter, D.L., & Prentky, R.A. (1989.) A system for the classification of child molesters. *Journal of Interpersonal Violence, 1*, 3-23.

Prentky, R.A., Knight, R.A., Rosenberg, R., & Lee, A. (1989) A path analytic approach to the validation of a taxonomic system for classifying child molesters. *Journal of Quantitative Criminology, 5*, 231-257.

Prentky, R.A., Knight, R.A., & Lee, A.F.S. (1997). Risk factors associated with recidivism among extrafamilial child molesters. *Journal of Consulting and Clinical Psychology, 65*, 141-149.

Quinsey, V.L., Lalumière, M., Rice, M.E., & Harris, G.T. (1995). Predicting sexual offenses. In J.C. Campbell (Ed.), *Assessing dangerousness* (pp. 114-137). Thousand Oaks, CA: Sage.

Radzinowicz, L. (1957). *Sexual offenses*. London: MacMillan.

Raymond, N.C., Coleman, E., Ohlerking, F., Christenson, G.A., & Miner, M. (1999). Psychiatric comorbidity in pedophilic sex offenders. *American Journal of Psychiatry, 156*, 786-788.

Schwenkmezger, P., Hodapp,V., & Spielberger, C.D. (1991) *Das State-Trait-Ärgerausdrucks-Inventar STAXI: Handbuch*. Bern, Göttingenn, Toronto: Huber.

Spielberger, C.D., Gorsuch, R.L., & Lushene, R.E. (1970). *STAI, Manual for the State-Trait-Anxiety-Inventory*. Palo Alto: Consulting Psychologists Press.

Stangier, U., & Heidenreich, T. (1997). Diagnostik der Sozialen Phobie. *Verhaltenstherapie, 7*, 107-118.

Sturgeon, V.H., & Taylor, J. (1980). Report of a five-year follow-up study of mentally disordered sex offenders released from Atascadero State Hospital in 1973. *Criminal Justice Journal, 4*, 31-63.

Wittchen, H-U., Wunderlich, U., Gruschwitz, S., & Zaudig, M. (1997). *SKID-I. Strukturiertes Klinisches Interview für DSM-IV*. Göttingen: Hogrefe.

Somatic and Mental Symptoms of Male Sex Offenders: A Comparison Among Offenders, Victims, and Their Families

L. C. Miccio-Fonseca, PhD

SUMMARY. This study explores whether or not somatic and mental symptoms differentiate male sex offenders from others by self-report. The present study was a part of a comprehensive, seven-year (1986-1993) research project described elsewhere (Miccio-Fonseca, 2000, 1996). In the present study there were three groups: male sex offenders ($N = 269$), victims (males, $N = 19$) and family members who were in neither category (males, $N = 64$). The groups were compared with regard to their reporting experiencing somatic and mental symptoms over the last six months.

Sex offenders, victims, and their family members differed on fourteen self-reported mental symptoms. Sex offenders rated themselves higher on symptoms dealing with cognitive difficulties, and victims described themselves as experiencing more complaints regarding mood difficulties. *[Article copies available for a fee from The Haworth Document Delivery Service: 1-800-HAWORTH. E-mail address: <getinfo@haworthpressinc.com> Website: <http://www.HaworthPress.com> © 2001 by The Haworth Press, Inc. All rights reserved.]*

KEYWORDS. Sex offenders, victims, brain, neuropsychological, mental symptoms, somatic symptoms, sex disorder, paraphilic disorder, paraphilia

---

L. C. Miccio-Fonseca is affiliated with the Clinic for the Sexualities.

[Haworth co-indexing entry note]: "Somatic and Mental Symptoms of Male Sex Offenders: A Comparison Among Offenders, Victims, and Their Families." Miccio-Fonseca, L. C. Co-published simultaneously in *Journal of Psychology & Human Sexuality* (The Haworth Press, Inc.) Vol. 13, No. 3/4, 2001, pp. 103-114; and: *Sex Offender Treatment: Accomplishments, Challenges, and Future Directions* (ed: Michael H. Miner, and Eli Coleman) The Haworth Press, Inc., 2001, pp. 103-114. Single or multiple copies of this article are available for a fee from The Haworth Document Delivery Service [1-800-HAWORTH, 9:00 a.m. - 5:00 p.m. (EST). E-mail address: getinfo@haworthpressinc.com].

Neuropsychological factors are rarely considered in the field of sex offenders. This is evidenced by the dearth of information and lack of mention in most research done on sex offenders, as well as in most psychological assessments and evaluations. These neuropsychological factors are equally absent the research on recidivism, risk, and the treatment of sex offenders (Abel, Mittelman, & Becker, 1985; Abel, Becker, & Skinner, 1985; Becker, Kaplin, Cunningham-Rathner, & Kavoussi, 1986; Cooper, Murphy, & Haynes, 1996; Davis & Leitenberg, 1987; Deisher, Wenet, Paperny, Clark, & Fehrenbach, 1982; Fehrenbach & Monastersky, 1988; Greenfeld, 1997; Groth, 1977; Groth & Birnbaum, 1978; Groth & Birnbaum, 1979; Hanson & Bussiere, 1996; Hanson & Bussiere, 1998; Kaplan & Green, 1995; Levin & Stava, 1987; Marshall & Barbaree, 1990; Marques, Nelson, West, & Day, 1994; Mathews, Hunter, & Vuz, 1997; O'Connor, 1987; Scavo, 1989; Wormith, 1985). Emerging research is demonstrating that the future may lie in making a closer examination of the neuropsychological factors and dynamics of the sex offender.

Researchers have compared and found differences among sex offenders with non-sex offenders with regard to brain functioning by using a variety of methods in modern medical technology (Langevin et al., 1989). Aigner et al. (2000) found that there was an association between unspecified brain anomalies and high violent behavior in their whole sample, as well as in the sex offender group. Other researchers found structural anomalies amongst pedophiles as seen on CT scans particularly in the left frontal-temporal area of the brain (Wright, Nobrega, Langevin, & Wortzman, 1990). Fruehwald et al. (2000) found higher rates of minimal brain abnormalities detected by Magnetic Resonance Imaging (MRI) among a sample of highly violent incarcerated sexual offenders compared to a low violence group.

Other research in the field of sex offenders has shown that pedophiles as a group suffer neuro-cognitive deficits as measured by the Halstead-Reitan Battery and the Luria Nebraska Neuropsychological Test Batteries (Langevin, Hucker, Ben-Aron, Purins, & Hook, 1985). Researchers have evidence that epilepsy brain damage and/or dysfunction appear to be significant in the beginning of unusual sexual behaviors (Langevin, 1990). Recent research suggests that there quite possibly may be a multifaceted interaction between learning disabilities, brain damage or dysfunction, and the presence of a sexual anomaly (Langevin, 1996; Langevin & Pope, 1993; Langevin et al., 1989; Hucker et al., 1988). What may seemingly appear as nonexistent for those sex offenders (and non-sex offenders) who suffer from Paraphilia Disorder (or other paraphilic related disorders), manifesting unconventional sexual behaviors may be in fact symptomatic of an early stage of a specific brain disorder that has yet to be identified.

The current investigation was intended to see whether or not male sex offenders reported an identifiable constellation of both somatic and mental symptoms that separates them from other groups. This study was a part of a comprehensive, seven-year (1986-1993) research project described elsewhere (Miccio-Fonseca, 1996, 2000). The larger project compared an array of variables, including psychological, medical, gynecological, urological, drug, law enforcement, homicidal and suicidal histories, and somatic and mental symptoms. Other variables studied were sexual difficulties and dysfunctions, sexual health, and life stressors.

METHOD

Subjects

The present study was a part of a comprehensive, seven-year (1986-1993) research project described elsewhere (Miccio-Fonseca, 2000, 1996). The total sample in that study was 656 people, of which 423 (64%) were males and 233 (36%) were females. They ranged from 4 to 71 years of age. There were 396 families in the data set. There were no significant differences among the group with regard to ethnic representation. The ethnic composition of the sample was 54% Caucasian, 24% Hispanic, 12% African-American, 2% Native American, 2% Asian and 6% other.

Usable data on somatic and mental symptoms were obtained from 352 respondents. In this study there were three groups, male sex offenders ($N = 269$), victims ($N = 19$) and individuals in neither category ($N = 64$). They were compared with regard to their reporting experiencing somatic and mental symptoms over the last six months. Each subject was interviewed for a minimum of 90 minutes. Sex offenders in the study were not in prison.

Subjects in the study were all from southern California (San Diego). They were either self-referred or referred by a law-enforcement official (probation officer, attorney, or judge) or by Child Protective Services. There were various reasons and purposes for the referral, consisting of psychotherapeutic treatment, consultation, or psychological assessment and evaluation.

Materials

In this study each individual completed an encyclopedic Male Intake Questionnaire, a self-report instrument that consisted of 183 items. The Male Intake Questionnaire form covered a variety of areas with regard to the person's psychological, medical, urological, gynecological, drug, law enforcement, psychiatric illness, homicidal and suicidal histories, and somatic symptoms and mental symptoms. Other items in the questionnaires cover sexual health, sexual difficulties and sexual dysfunctions. The questionnaires include a number of items based on the Holmes-Rahe scale (Holmes & Rahe, 1967), asking the respondent to check the life-stress events experienced during the preceding 12 months.

The purpose of the Male Intake Questionnaire was to obtain a comprehensive picture of the individual clinically, particularly with regard to sexuality. Since these data were collected as part of clinical practice and not specifically for a research study, informed consent was not necessary. There was no "treatment effect" being tested in this *post hoc* analysis of these clinical data.

The somatic and mental symptoms items were solicited from researchers who were a group of specialists (two psychologists, two reproductive endocrinologists) in the area of menstrual-cycle functioning and sexual trauma. This group produced a list of 150 symptoms that were related to general medical and psychological history. These were generated from interview protocols from clinical practice over a four-year period.

Each of the items on the symptoms list was then rated by respondents according to how intensely he experienced the symptom. This symptom list has been utilized in different forms, one of which included development of the Premenstrual Experience Assessment Tool (Futterman et al., 1988). The questionnaire was later modified for research in the area of sexual abuse and sex offenders (Futterman et al., 1992; Miccio-Fonseca, 1990; Miccio-Fonseca, 1996, 2000).

Procedures

A licensed psychologist interviewed each individual in a clinical setting. The psychologist specialized in the Paraphilia Disorder, as defined in the *Diagnostic and Statistical Manual of Mental Disorders-IV*. Individual interviews varied in length from a minimum of 90 minutes to several hours.

In this study "sex offender" is defined as a male who either has admitted to, or been convicted of, a sex crime or has encountered legal difficulties such as allegations, arrests, convictions and/or custody because
of sexual habits other than prostitution. This definition covers such offenses as incest, rape, molestation, exhibitionism, and peeping. "Victim" is defined as a person who has reported experiencing sexual abuse
(e.g., exhibitionism, incest, rape, or molestation). Individuals in "neither category" are members of the families of sex offenders who were
neither victims nor sex offenders themselves.

Subjects who could not read English or were otherwise unable to
complete the questionnaire were given one of the two forms of the questionnaire through structured interviews. Subjects who could complete
the questionnaire on their own were also interviewed. All of the data
presented in this paper were from direct interview. Each questionnaire
item was reviewed and explored with each subject, and additional data
were gathered in the process.

STATISTICAL ANALYSIS

Chi-square analyses were carried out on all categorical data. This
procedure "corrected" for uneven $N's$. Alpha was set at 0.05 for all tests
of significance. Since numerous (117) chi square tests were carried out,
the Bonoferoni adjustment reduced the alpha to 0.001, to guard against
Type 1 errors. There were two degrees of freedom for each chi square test
of significance. All comparisons reported represent statistically significant differences; non-significant differences are not reported.

The statistical inferences do not, of course, reflect the general population. The samples, although ones of convenience, probably represent
sub-populations of people who are victims of sexual crimes, who are
sex offenders, or who are members of families that include sex offenders or victims. No attempt was made to estimate the incidence of sex offense within the population of people in general, since the offenders,
victims, and family samples were either self-referred or referred by a
law-enforcement official, and because of the high probability that such
offenses are underreported.

RESULTS

There were no statistically significant findings on any of the 58 somatic items. The three groups differed significantly on 14 of the mental

symptoms (see Table 1). In order to explore trends in the chi-square tables, the data were collapsed to include all responses of "Some," "Frequent," and "Quite a bit" expressed as percentage of total responses to the items.

In Table 1, mental symptoms, the percentages are rank-ordered from high to low for sex offenders, with corresponding percentages for the other two groups. Of the 54 statistically significant comparisons on mental symptoms, sex offenders were highest on 14 symptoms. Sex offenders and victims tied on Poor Concentration and Difficulty Thinking Clearly. In general, sex offenders reported relatively high ratings on the following fourteen symptoms: Feeling Depressed, Feeling Shame, Easily Distracted, Feeling Lonely, Poor Concentration, Feeling Alone, Poor Judgment, Difficulty Thinking Clearly, Acting Impulsively, Feeling Isolated, Difficulty Making Decisions, Inability to Plan Ahead, Withdrawal from Others, and Decrease in Sexual Interest. The lowest percentage was on the item of Outbursts of Anger. The percentage for victims who reported having Outbursts of Anger was in notable contrast: at 76% versus 15%.

DISCUSSION

The male sex offenders in this study were not sex offenders from a prison setting. This study investigated whether or not male sex offenders report a constellation of both somatic and mental symptoms that sets them apart from others.

There were no statistically significant findings on the 58 somatic items. A possible reason for there being no somatic differences is that these individuals may not be valid reporters of measure of somatic symptoms. That is, somatic symptoms may be less powerful than mental symptoms. Another possible reason might be that these people may be more reluctant to report somatic symptoms than mental symptoms. Some people may be embarrassed by what is going on in their bodies and not likely to report these concerns and/or symptoms. It may also be that individuals, if physically traumatized, can have lasting effects that contaminate self-report with regard to somatic symptoms.

These individuals may also experience mistrust of any kind of intrusion of their body privacy, they may become defensive, or there may be researcher effect. The researcher effect may be influenced by the fact that the researcher is asking questions face to face, and this may produce a response that may impact how these individuals are reacting to

TABLE 1. Self-Reported Mental Symptoms of Male Sex Offenders, Male Victims, and Males in Neither Category

Symptom	Percentage Reporting Some or More			Chi Square
	Sex Offenders $N = 269$	Victims $N = 19$	Neither Category $N = 64$	
Feeling depressed	54	39	20	23.939
Feeling shame	48	6	11	35.027
Easily distracted	47	37	16	14.126
Feeling lonely	47	23	15	23.543
Poor concentration	44	44	16	17.278
Feeling alone	43	29	16	16.858
Poor judgment	40	28	11	18.367
Difficulty thinking clearly	39	39	11	18.422
Acting impulsively	38	32	11	15.815
Feeling isolated	36	13	11	16.351
Difficulty making decisions	36	33	11	14.381
Inability to plan ahead	35	33	11	13.438
Withdrawal from others	30	36	5	15.380
Decrease in sexual interest	20	0	2	14.872
Outbursts of anger	15	76	20	19.323

the interview. They may fear that if they report having somatic symptoms, they may be judged. The researcher effect may also exist by virtue of a psychologist interviewing these individuals who may have believed that it was more important to report mental symptoms; if they were talking to a medical doctor, they may be more forthcoming about somatic symptoms.

The findings on the mental symptoms, however, were significant. The sex offender's self-reports showed a constellation of 14 specific mental symptoms that differed from those of the other compared groups of males in this study. The findings suggest that male sex offenders may have something distinctly different going on in their brains from that of others.

Examining the constellation of symptoms reported, one finds a variety of possible disorders. For example, the symptoms of feeling depressed, withdrawal from others, poor concentration, difficulty making decisions, inability to plan ahead, and decrease in sexual interest, may be indicative of an Affective Disorder. Mood disorders like depression can be treated with anti-depressants. Like a domino effect, the antidepressants have specific actions on serotonin which effect norepinephrine, which may also influence the regulation of the stress system. Professionals working with sex offenders are well aware of stress levels being a variable that the sex offender needs to monitor to reduce risk of recidivism. The findings in this study support further research in these areas.

The symptoms of poor concentration, easily distracted, difficulty thinking clearly, difficulty making decisions, and acting impulsively may be indicative of impairment in the attentional system of the individual. Individuals with attentional dysfunction have an inability to dispense cognitive resources effectively to the tasks at hand, and fail to perform at optimal level even though primary cognitive resources, such as sensory registration, perception, memory and associative functions are intact. Individuals with primary attentional disorders are able to perceive sensory input, comprehend language, form and retrieve memories and perform other cognitive functions, yet they fail to do so consistently.

Another possibility is that the symptoms of depressive symptoms, poor concentration, easily distracted, difficulty thinking clearly, and acting impulsively may be indicative of dissociative problems and/or related to dissociative disorders. Those seasoned working with sex offenders are familiar with their frequently reporting having difficulty recalling the specifics of some of their sex offense behaviors and/or "don't remember" these events. This particular possibility, that these symptoms are related to dissociative disorders, may be more prevalent than is currently recognized in the field and may come to be one of the important variables that are related to paraphilic behaviors and/or Paraphilia Disorder.

Attentional disturbances and dissociative disorders have been related to affective disorders as well as connected with frontal lobe and executive functions which in turn have been related to social controls (Kolb & Whishaw, 1998; Snyder & Nussbaum, 1998). Executive functions involve a number of abilities that are directly related to treatment and positive treatment outcome. The executive functions include abilities such as the ability to formulate goals with regard for long-term consequences, the ability to generate multiple response alternatives, the ability to choose and initiate goal-directed behaviors, the ability to self-regulate and adequately correct the behavior, the ability of correcting and modifying behaviors when conditions change and the ability of being able to persevere in the face of distraction (Kolb & Whishaw, 1998; Snyder & Nussbaum, 1998).

The reported constellation of mental symptoms that were isolated in this study of male sex offenders suggests consideration of exploring or ruling out possible neurological and/or neuro-psychological disorders. The constellation of mental symptoms may indicate a prodromal state amongst sex offenders, which may be useful information when diagnosing a sex disorder amongst sex offenders or for treating the disorder. It is possible that unconventional sexual behavior may be symptomatic of the early stage of a brain disease that may manifest itself later. These proposed clinical possibilities relating the symptoms that sex offenders reported and their relationship to a particular disorder needs to be further investigated and explored. Additional research is needed to establish these connections scientifically as well as treatments for such disorders if found present.

The findings in this study call for the development of new treatment and assessment paradigms in the field of male sex offenders. Such new models should be more inclusive and comprehensive, consistently including the consideration of neuropsychological factors of the sex offender. The currently existing paradigms in the field of sex offenders primarily concentrate on the behavioral *manifestations* of brain functioning and not the functioning itself. Inferences about brain functioning from behavioral manifestations are open to unreliable interpretations. Any new model with regard to the assessment and treatment of sex offenders should include other factors such as neuropsychological variables, hormones, and sexual anomalies.

There are limitations in this study, one of which is that the researcher conducted the clinical interviews. This practice of data gathering could have a contaminating effect. Further research could include alternative data-collection methods and more objective data gathering. Another limitation of the study is the use of self-reports of sexual behavior and personal history. It is for the most part unknowable whether sex offenders are completely forthcoming with regard to their own histories. A majority of people in this study claimed to have been victims of sexual abuse themselves. Such claims, of course, could be attempts to minimize their responsibilities with regard to their own offenses. Their reports of suicide attempts may also have been, to some degree, a way of masking personal culpability.

Another limitation of this study was that no standard neuro-psychological test or standardized symptom checklist was used.

REFERENCES

Abel, G., Mittelman, M.S., & Becker, J. (1985). Sexual offenders: Results of assessment and recommendations for treatment. In H. H. Ben-Aron, S. I. Hucker, & C.D. Webster (Eds.), *Clinical criminology* (pp. 191-205). Toronto, Ontario, Canada: MM Graphics.

Abel, G.G., Barlow, D.H., Blanchard, E.B., & Guild, D. (1977). The components of rapists' sexual arousal. *Archives of General Psychiatry, 34*, 895-903.

Abel, G.G., Becker, J.V., & Skinner, L.J. (1985). Behavioral approaches to treatment of the violent sex offender. In L.H. Roth (Eds.), *Clinical treatment of the violent person*. Rockville, MD: National Institute of Mental Health.

Aigner, Martin, Eher, Reinhard, Fruehwald, S., Frottier, Patrick, K., Guiterrez-Lobos, S., & Dwyer, Margretta (2000). Brain abnormalities and violent behavior. Special Edition, *Journal of Psychology & Human Sexuality, 11*(3).

Bain, J., Langevin, R., Dickey, R., Hucker, S., & Wright, P. (1988). Hormones in sexually aggressive men. *Annals of Sex Research, 1*, 443-454.

Bain, J., Langevin, R., Hucker, S., Dickey, R., & Wright, P. & Schonberg, C. (1988). Sex hormones in pedophiles. *Annals of Sex Research, 1*, 63-78.

Barbaree, H., & Marshall, W.L. (1988). Deviant arousal, offense history and demographic variables as predictors of re-offense among child molesters. *Behavioral Sciences & the Law, 6*, 267-280.

Barbaree, H., Marshall, W.L., & Lanthier, R. (1979). Deviant sexual arousal in rapists. *Behavior Research & Therapy, 17*, 215-22.

Becker, J.V., Kaplin, M.S., Cunningham-Rathner, J., & Kavoussi, R. (1986). Characteristics of adolescent incest sexual perpetrators: Preliminary findings. *Journal of Family Violence, 1*, 85-97.

Bradford, J.M.W. (1995). Pharmacological treatment of the Paraphilia. In J. M. Oldham & M. B. Riva (Eds.), *American Psychiatric Press Review of Psychiatry, Vol. 14*. Washington, DC: American Psychiatric Press.

Carroll, B.J., Curtis, G.C., & Mendels, J. (1976). Neuro-endocrine regulation in depression. II. Discrimination of depressed from non-depressed patients. *Archives of General Psychiatry*, 33:1051-1058.

Cooper, C., Murphy W.D., & Haynes, M.R. (1996). Characteristics of abused and nonabused adolescent sexual offenders. *Sexual Abuse: A Journal of Research and Treatment, 8*(2), 105-119.

Davis, G.L., & Leitenberg, H. (1987). Adolescent sex offenders. *Psychological Bulletin, 101* (3), 417-427.

Deisher, R.W., Wenet, G.A., Paperny, D.M., Clark, T.F., & Fehrenbach, P.A. (1982). Adolescent sex offense behavior: The role of the physician. *Journal of Adolescent Health Care, 2*, 279-286.

Diagnostic and statistical manual of mental disorders. Fourth Edition. (1994). Washington, DC: American Psychiatric Association.

Fehrenbach, P.A., & Monastersky, C. (1988). Characteristics of female adolescent sexual offenders. *American Journal of Orthopsychiatry, 58* (1).

Fehrenbach, P.A., Smith, W., Monastersky, C., & Deisher, R.W. (1986). Adolescent sexual offenders: Offender and offense characteristics. *American Journal of Orthopsychiatry, 56*, 225-233.

Flor-Henry, P. (1987). Cerebral aspects of sexual deviation. In G.D. Wilson (Ed.), *Variant sexuality: Research and theory*. Beechenham, Kent, England: Croom Helm Ltd.

Flor-Henry, P., Lang, R., Koles, Z.J., & Frenzel, R.R. (1988). Quantitative EEG investigations of genital exhibitionists. *Annals of Sex Research, 1*, 49-62.

Fruehwald, Stefan, Eher, Reinhard, Frottier, Patrick, & Aigner, Martin. (2000). Self-concepts and interpersonal perceptions of sexual offenders in relation to brain abnormalities. *Special Edition, Journal of Psychology & Human Sexuality, 11*(3).

Futterman, L.A., Jones, John E., Miccio-Fonseca, L.C., & Quigley, M.E. Ted (1992). Severity of Premenstrual Symptoms in Relation to Medical/Psychiatric Problems and Life Experiences. *Perceptual and Motor Skills, Vol. 74*, pp. 787-799.

Futterman, L.A., Jones, John E., Miccio-Fonseca, L.C., & Quigley, M.E. Ted (1988). Assessing premenstrual syndrome using the premenstrual experience assessment. *Psychological Reports, 63*, 19-34.

Greenfeld, L.A. (NCJ-163392, February 1997). *Sex offenses and offenders: An analysis of data on rape and sexual assault*. Washington, DC: U.S. Department of Justice, Office of Justice Programs, Bureau of Justice Statistics.

Groth, N.A. (1977). The adolescent sexual offender and his prey. *International Journal of Offender Therapy and Comparative Criminology, 21*, 249-254.

Groth, N.A., & Birnbaum, H.J. (1978). Adult sexual orientation and attraction to underage persons. *Archives of Sexual Behavior, 7*, 175-181.

Groth, N.A., & Birnbaum, H.J. (1979). *Men who rape: The psychology of the offender*. New York: Plenum Press.

Hanson, R.K., & Bussière, M.T. (1996). Predictors of sexual offender recidivism: A meta-analysis. Ottawa, Ontario: Ministry of the Solicitor General of Canada.

Hanson, R.K., & Bussière, M.T. (1998). Predicting relapse: A meta-analysis of sex offender recidivism studies. *Journal of Consulting and Clinical Psychology, 66* (2), 348-362.

Healy, D. (1987). Rhythm and blues. Neurochemical, neuro-pharmacological and neuropsychological implications of a hypothesis of circadian rhythm dysfunction in the affective disorders. *Psychopharmacology, 93*: 271-285.

Hucker, S., Langevin, R., & Bain, J. (1988). A double bind trial of Provera for pedophiles. *Annals of Sex Research, 1*, 227-242.

Kaplan, M.S., & Green, A. (1995). Incarcerated female sexual offender: A comparison of sexual histories with eleven female nonsexual offenders. *Sexual Abuse: A Journal of Research and Treatment, 7(4)*, 287-300.

Kolb, B., & Whishaw, I. (1998). *Fundamentals of human neuropsychology*. 4th Edition, New York: W.H. Freeman and Co.

Langevin, R. (1996). Major factors n the assessment of paraphilics and sex offenders. *Journal of Offender Rehabilitation, 23*(3-4), 1996.

Langevin, R., Wright, P., & Handy, L. (1989). Characteristics of sex offenders who were sexually victimized as children. *Annals of Sex Research, 2*, 227-254.

Langevin, R., Lang, R., Wortzman, G., Frenzel, R., & Wright, P. (1989). An examination of brain damage and dysfunction in genital exhibitionists. *Annals of Sex Research, 2*, 77-88.

Langevin, R., Wortzman, G., Wright, P., & Handy, L. (1989). Studies of brain damage and dysfunction in sex offenders. *Annals of Sex Research, 2,* 163-179.

Langevin, R., & Pope, S. (1993). Working with learning disabled sex offenders. *Annals of Sex Research.*

Langevin, R., Hucker, S.J., Ben-Aron, M.H., Purins, J.E., & Hook, H.J. (1985). In R. Langevin (Ed.), *Erotic preference, gender identity, and aggression in men: New research studies* (pp. 181-210). Hillsdale, NJ: Lawrence Erlbaum Associates.

Levin, S. M., & Stava, L. (1987). Personality characteristics of sex offenders: A review. *Archives of Sexual Behavior, 16,* 57-59.

Marques, J., Nelson, C., West, M.A., & Day, D.M. (1994). The relationship between treatment goals and recidivism among child molesters. *Behavior Research & Therapy, 32*(5), 577-588.

Marshall, W.L., & Barbaree, H.E. (1990). Outcome of comprehensive cognitive-behavioral treatment programs. In W.L., Marshall, D.R. Laws, & H.E. Barbaree (Eds.), *Handbook of sexual assault: Issues, theories and treatment of the offender* (pp. 363-385). New York: Plenum Press.

Mathews, R., Hunter, J., & Vuz, J. (1997). Juvenile female sexual offenders: Clinical characteristics and treatment issues. *Sexual Abuse: A Journal of Research and Treatment, 9*(3), 187-200.

Miccio-Fonseca, L.C. (2000). Adult and adolescent female sex offenders: Experiences compared to other females and male sex offenders. *Special Edition, Journal of Psychology & Human Sexuality, 11*(3).

Miccio-Fonseca, L.C. (1998). *Sex, brain, and sex offenders.* Clinic for The Sexualities, San Diego, CA.

Miccio-Fonseca, L.C. (1996). Comparative differences in psychological histories of sex offenders, victims and their families. *Journal of Offender Rehabilitation, 23*(3-4), 1996.

O'Connor, A.A. (1987). Female sex offenders. *British Journal of Psychiatry, 150,* 615-620.

Ross, E.D., & Rush, A.J. (1981). Diagnosis and neuroanatomical correlates of depression in brain-damaged patients. *Archives of General Psychiatry, 38:* 1344-1354.

Scavo, R. (1989). Female sex offenders: A neglected treatment group. *The Journal of Contemporary Social Work,* pp. 114-117.

Snyder, P.J. & Nussbaum, P.D. (1998). *Clinical neuropsychology.* American Psychological Association, Washington, DC.

Wormith, J.S. (1985). Some physiological and cognitive aspects of assessing deviant sexual arousal. Report No. 1985-26. Ottawa: Ministry of the Solicitor General of Canada.

Wright, P., Nobrega, J., Langevin, R., & Wortzman, G. (1990). Brain density and symmetry in pedophiles and sexually aggressive men. *Annals of Sex Research, 3,* 319-328.

Standards of Care for the Treatment
of Adult Sex Offenders

Eli Coleman, PhD
S. Margretta Dwyer, MA
Gene Abel, MD
Wolfgang Berner, MD
James Breiling, PhD
Reinhard Eher, MD
Jan Hindman, MA
Ron Langevin, PhD
Thore Langfeldt, PhD
Michael H. Miner, PhD
Friedemann Pfäfflin, MD
Peter Weiss, PhD

SUMMARY. A proposed version of these standards was first produced
and published in the *Journal of Offender Rehabilitation* through input
from professional meetings (Coleman & Dwyer, 1990). Since that time,
The Standards of Care were reviewed and revised by a group of professionals and unanimously endorsed by voice vote by the participants in the
Third International Congress on the Treatment of Sex Offenders held in
Minneapolis, MN, September 20-22, 1994. These Standards were again

---

Address correspondence to: Eli Coleman, PhD, Professor and Director, Program in
Human Sexuality, School of Medicine, University of Minnesota, 1300 S. 2nd Street,
Suite 180, Minneapolis, MN 55454 USA (E-mail: colem001@tc.umn.edu).

[Haworth co-indexing entry note]: "Standards of Care for the Treatment of Adult Sex Offenders."
Coleman et al. Co-published simultaneously in *Journal of Psychology & Human Sexuality* (The Haworth
Press, Inc.) Vol. 13, No. 3/4, 2001, pp. 115-121; and: *Sex Offender Treatment: Accomplishments, Challenges,
and Future Directions* (ed: Michael H. Miner, and Eli Coleman) The Haworth Press, Inc., 2001, pp. 115-121.
Single or multiple copies of this article are available for a fee from The Haworth Document Delivery Service
[1-800-HAWORTH, 9:00 a.m. - 5:00 p.m. (EST). E-mail address: getinfo@haworthpressinc.com].

published in the *Journal of Offender Rehabilitation* (Coleman, Dwyer, Abel, Berner, Breiling, Hindman, Honey-Knopp, Langevin, & Pfäfflin, 1996). Those Standards have been subsequently reviewed by the current authors at the Fifth International Conference on the Treatment of Sex Offenders held in Caracas, Venezuela, March 22-27, 1998 and minor modifications and changes were incorporated into this version. The authors invite feedback from readers. Further revisions are anticipated and will be reviewed by current committee members and at future International Conferences on the Treatment of Sexual Offenders. *[Article copies available for a fee from The Haworth Document Delivery Service: 1-800-HAWORTH. E-mail address: <getinfo@haworthpressinc.com> Website: <http://www.HaworthPress.com> © 2001 by The Haworth Press, Inc. All rights reserved.]*

KEYWORDS. Sexual offenders, sexual offenses, assessment, treatment, standards of care, guidelines

A paraphilia is a condition of compulsive response to, or dependence upon, an unusual and unacceptable stimulus in the imagery of fantasy, for optimal initiation and fantasy during solo masturbation or sexual activity with a partner. There are well over 40 types of paraphilias which have been identified and defined (Money, 1986). Only eight of them are listed in the *Diagnostic and Statistical Manual of Mental Disorders* (American Psychiatric Association, 1994), where the remainder are subsumed under, "not otherwise specified." Given the sociocultural-religious-political climate, some paraphilias are legally considered to be sex crimes which are punishable by law. In legal codes, crimes against nature and affronts to socially acceptable sexual behavior are criminalized and are regarded as sexual offenses. These crimes have included statutory rape, violent rape, child molesting, exhibitionism, voyeurism and incest. What is considered a sexual crime and the standards of punishment are state, time, and culture dependent. Over time, there have been many revisions of the criminal sexual codes (Pallone, 1990).

For the most part, today sexual offenders may be fined, ordered to psychological or medical treatment, and/or imprisoned. For first-time offenders, and for lesser offenses, there is a greater likelihood of probation, subject to some specific professional sexual offender treatment.

Although treatment is costly and unaffordable by some, not to treat can be more costly emotionally and psychologically for the offender, for the victims and future victims, and for society. The predominant view of the lay public around the world is that sexual crimes can be eradicated with punishment, indeterminate incarceration and/or death. This predominant view is not supported by scientific evidence, and the scientific community needs to continue to promote awareness that sexual crimes can be the manifestations of biomedical/psychiatric/psychological illnesses for which people must be treated, rather than simply punished.

In recent decades, the demand for sexual offender treatment has increased, as have the number and variety of possible biomedical/psychiatric/psychological treatments. The rationale upon which such treatments have been offered has become more and more complex. Various "appropriate care" philosophies have been suggested by many professionals who have identified themselves as experts on the topic of sexual offenders.

In an effort to establish minimal acceptable guidelines for the treatment of sexual offenders, the authors present the following Standards of Care as guidelines, which might be helpful to enhance the ethical and professional treatment of sexual offenders throughout the world.

STATEMENT OF PURPOSE

Although each profession has its own standards of care, the following are minimal recommendations of Standards of Care. It is recommended that professionals involved in the treatment of sexual offenders use the following *minimal criteria* for the evaluation of their work. It is recommended that the reasons for exceptions to these standards, in the management of any individual case, be very carefully documented.

DEFINITIONS

Standards of Care

Standards of Care are exactly what is implied: standards for caring for patients. In this case: care and treatment of sexual offenders.

Paraphilia

Paraphilia is an erotosexual condition occurring in men and women who are responsive to, or dependent upon, an unusual or socially unacceptable stimulus in imagery or fantasy for initiation and maintenance of erotic-sexual arousal and the facilitation or attainment of orgasm.

Sexual Offense

A sexual offense involves engaging in illegal sexual behavior which is defined by criminal statutes. It should also be noted that there is great discrepancy throughout the world as to what constitutes a sexual offense (Pallone, 1990).

Sexual Offender

An individual who commits a sexual crime as legally defined in his or her own culture's legal jurisdiction is a sexual offender.

Psychological Treatment

Psychological treatment refers to the array of therapies which have been designed to treat sexual offenders. Different treatments are based on different psychological and psychiatric theories regarding the origin of the paraphilic sexual offending, for example, psychoanalytic, cognitive, behavioral, social learning, and family systems theories. Psychological or psychiatric care can be provided in individual, couple, family or group settings. The purpose of treatment is to prevent further offending behavior and further victimization of others.

Biomedical Treatment

Biomedical treatment refers to the use of pharmacological treatment. Pharmacologic therapy has included (but is not limited to) the use of antiandrogens, antidepressants, and antianxiety, antiepileptic, antipsychotic, and/or other medications.

PROFESSIONAL COMPETENCE

Possession of an academic degree in behavioral science, medicine, or for the provision of psychosocial clinical services does not necessarily attest to the possession of sufficient competence to conduct assessment or treatment of paraphilic or sexual offending problems. Persons assessing and/or treating sexual offenders should have clinical training and experience in the diagnosis and treatment of a range of psychiatric and psychological conditions and also specialized training and experience in the assessment and treatment of paraphilic and sexual offender problems. This would generally be reflected by appropriate licensure as a psychiatrist, psychologist, or clinical therapist and by documentation of training and experience in the diagnosis and treatment of a broad range of sexual conditions, including paraphilic disorders and sexual offenses. Treatment providers must be competent in making a differential diagnosis.

The following *minimal standards* for a professional should be adhered to:

1. A minimum of a master's degree or its equivalent or medical degree in a clinical field granted by an institution of education accredited by a national/regional accrediting board or institution.
2. Demonstrated competence in therapy and indicated by a license (or its equivalent from a certifying body) to practice medicine, psychology, clinical social work, professional counseling, or marriage and family counseling.
3. Demonstrated specialized competence in counseling and diagnosis of sexual disorders and sexual offending behaviors as documentable by training or supervised clinical experience, along with continuing education.
4. Demonstrated training and competence in providing psychotherapy.

ANTECEDENTS TO SEXUAL OFFENDER TREATMENT

1. Prospective patients should receive an extensive evaluation of their sexual offending behavior and their overall sexual health. It would also include appropriateness for treatment, amenability for treatment, psychological/psychiatric diagnoses, and evaluation for the safety and protection of the community.
2. A thorough physical examination is recommended especially when physical problems are suspected that might require specific treatment, i.e., heart problems, high blood pressure, liver damage, brain lesions, and epilepsy.
3. Prospective patients should receive a psychological and/or psychiatric examination, which would rule out other psychological/psychiatric disorders. If any other psychological/psychiatric disorders are found, treatment of such disorder requires treatment

in addition to their treatment for their paraphilic or sexual offending behavior.

4. If medication is deemed necessary or requested by the patient, the patient must be given information regarding the benefits and potential side effects or disadvantages of biomedical treatment.

THE PRINCIPLES OF THE STANDARDS OF CARE

Principle 1: There is evidence that some kinds of treatment may be effective in managing and reducing recidivism with some types of sexual offenders.

Principle 2: Sexual offender treatment is viewed by offenders as an elective process (the choice is theirs), since individuals may not view their sexual offending behavior as psychologically or medically pathological.

Principle 3: The evaluation of treatment of sexual offenders requires specialized skills not usually associated with the professional training of clinical therapists or medical professionals.

Principle 4: Sexual offender treatment is performed for the purpose of improving quality of life and is considered a humane treatment for people who have committed a sexual offense; it is also performed to prevent the patient from engaging in further sexual offending behavior.

Principle 5: The patient with a documented biomedical abnormality is first treated by procedures commonly accepted as appropriate for any such medical conditions before beginning, or in conjunction with, psychotherapy.

Principle 6: The patient having a psychiatric diagnosis (i.e., schizophrenia) is first treated by procedures commonly accepted as appropriate for the psychiatric diagnoses, or if appropriate, for both.

Principle 7: Sexual offender treatment may involve a variety of therapeutic approaches. It is important for professionals to keep abreast of this growing and developing field and provide the most efficacious treatments, which have been demonstrated through outcome studies.

Principle 8: A treatment plan may involve the use of pharmacotherapy, which may relieve some sexual arousal and fantasy, and some individuals may feel less driven.

Principle 9: Professionals who work with sexual offenders should be prepared to work with the criminal justice system in a professional and cooperative manner.

Principle 10: Sexual offenders often have a need for follow-up treatment/visits, and this should be encouraged or possibly required.

Principle 11: It is unethical to charge patients for services, which are essentially for research or which do not directly benefit the patient.

Principle 12: In order to effectively persuade the professionals in the legal community as well as society in general about the efficacy of sexual offender treatment, professionals should cooperate with and carry out scientifically sound treatment outcome research.

Principle 13: Sexual offenders often must face legal proceedings, and professionals treating these individuals must be prepared to appear in court if necessary.

Principle 14: Sexual offenders are given the same rights to medical and psychological privacies as any other patient group, with the exception of where the law requires otherwise, i.e., reporting laws, subpoenaing of records.

Principle 15: Sexual offenders should not be discriminated against based on age, gender, race, ethnicity, national origin, religious beliefs, socioeconomic status, or physical or mental disability.

Principle 16: Professionals who treat sexual offenders must view these individuals with dignity and respect. If they fail to view the offender or their offense with compassion, then the professional should make a proper referral.

REFERENCES

American Psychiatric Association. (1994). *Diagnostic and Statistical Manual of the American Psychiatric Association (DSM-IV)*. Washington, DC: The American Psychiatric Association.

Coleman, E. & Dwyer, S. M. (1990). Proposed standards of care for the treatment of adult sex offenders. *Journal of Offender Rehabilitation, 16* (1/2), 93-106.

Coleman, E., Dwyer, S. M., Abel, G., Berner, W., Breiling, J., Hindman, J., Honey-Knopp, F., Langevin, R., & Pfäfflin, F. (1996). Standards of care for the treatment of adult sex offenders. *Journal of Offender Rehabilitation, 22* (3/4).

Money, J. (1986). *Lovemaps: Clinical Concepts of Sexual/Erotic Health & Pathology, Paraphilia, and Gender Transposition in Childhood, Adolescence & Maturity*. Buffalo: Prometheus.

Pallone, J. J. (1990). *Rehabilitating Criminal Sexual Psychopaths: Legislative Mandates. Clinical Quandaries*. New Brunswick, NJ: Transaction Books.

Index